CANDICE OLSON
KITCHENS & BATHS

PHOTOGRAPHS BY BRANDON BARRÉ

WILEY

Wiley Publishing, Inc.

For general information on our other products and services or to obtain technical support please contact our Customer Care Department within the U.S. at (877) 762-2974, outside the U.S. at (317) 572-3993 or fax (317) 572-4002.

Wiley also publishes its books in a variety of electronic formats. Some content that appears in print may not be available in electronic books. For more information about Wiley products, please visit our web site at www.wiley.com.

Library of Congress Control Number: 2011921779

ISBN: 978-0-470-88937-4 (pbk)

ISBN: 978-1-118-00493-7 (ebk)

Printed in the United States of America

10 9 8 7 6 5 4 3

Note to the Readers:
Due to differing conditions, tools and the individual skills, John Wiley & Sons, Inc. assumes no responsibility for any damages, injuries suffered, or losses incurred as a result of following the information published in this book. Before beginning any project, review the instructions carefully, and if any doubts or questions remain, consult local experts or authorities. Because codes and regulations vary greatly, you always should check with authorities to ensure that your project complies with all applicable local codes and regulations. Always read and observe all of the safety precautions provided by manufacturers of any tools, equipment, or supplies, and follow all accepted safety procedures.

Book design by Tai Blanche
Cover design by Susan Olinski

For my grandmother,

whose apron strings I tugged on more times

than I can count.

She may have passed on, but her recipe for

cherry cheesecake lives eternally!

Candice Olson is one of North America's leading designers and most recognized media personalities. Her long-running television series, *Divine Design with Candice Olson,* has been seen by millions of viewers around the world. Her newest show, *Candice Tells All,* features her signature room makeovers while giving viewers an inside look at her design process and inspiration.

After earning her degree from the School of Interior Design at Ryerson University in Toronto, Candice launched an exciting commercial and residential design business. Considered "the one to watch" by *The New York Times*, Candice continues to receive accolades and media attention for her distinctive and exceptional work.

Candice's foray into television began when a local TV station profiled one of her award-winning design projects. Her engaging personality and unique approach to residential design led to a weekly stint as a design contributor to the show. Viewer demand for "more Candice!" led to the creation of the hit series *Divine Design with Candice Olson*. Candice and the show quickly won a huge and loyal audience. Airing in more than 150 countries, *Divine Design with Candice Olson* continues to receive rave reviews and recognition from around the world.

In 2005, Candice launched the Candice Olson Collection, her own successful brand of licensed product lines, including upholstered furniture, fabrics, wallpaper, lighting, case goods, and bedding. Candice's signature style is one she describes as "a fusion of traditional form, scale, and proportions with the clean, crisp, simplistic beauty of modern design."

Candice has made guest appearances on television shows such as *Today*, *Live! with Regis and Kelly*, *The View*, and *The Oprah Winfrey Show*. She is regularly featured in newspapers and magazines throughout North America.

Candice spends her free time with her family, skiing in the winter and relaxing at the beach in summer. A native of Calgary, Alberta, she lives in Toronto with her husband and two children.

Visit www.candiceolsonkitchensandbaths.com to find detailed information about the materials and products from all of her spectacular kitchens and bathrooms found in this book.

Table of Contents

KITCHENS

Fabulous Family Spaces

2 Designed for Entertaining

BATHS

3 Master Suite Spaces

4 Relaxing Retreats

INTRODUCTION

Okay, so I know I might be biased, but my grandmother was *the* best cook! And I didn't know it as a little girl, but looking back, I realize she probably had one of the *worst* kitchens I've ever seen! Oh, if I only knew at the age of six what I know now.

Her humble farmhouse kitchen had a wood stove that acted as both furnace and kettle-boiler, a temperamental electric range, and barely enough counter space for my skinny behind to perch on and lick batter from the bowls. But it was here that my grandma prepared *the* most delicious meals! To complicate matters, her house lacked a separate dining room, so the tiny kitchen also had to play host to large family gatherings and sit-down dinners. I looked at it as glass-half-full: With barely an inch to move, it was always easy for someone to lean over and grab something from the fridge or oven without even standing up! And we kids had a permanent reservation at the exclusive "special table"—otherwise known as the ironing board!—which my grandma set to the side of the kitchen table. Between preparing and serving the meals, eating, and then cleaning up, the scene was utter chaos! It's no wonder that on more than one occasion, Grandma lost her culinary cool and threateningly wielded a spatula in the direction of anyone who dared come between her and her pot of carefully simmering cabbage rolls.

As much as this kitchen was dated and awkward, on another level, it was way ahead of its time. It was the social center of the house, where friends and family were always welcome to share good food and good times—a concept that has become the essence of modern-day kitchen design.

Today's kitchen is all about a well-planned space that makes cooking a completely interactive experience between family and friends. Popular open-concept planning puts the kitchen at center stage in the home, with meal prep, serving, and cleanup playing lead roles and providing the entertainment. This means that planning and design choices for the kitchen (and there are a lot of them!) are wide-reaching and extend to influence color, material, and even fabric and upholstery selections in the surrounding rooms. The kitchen remains to this day the most important room in the house and the project I am most often approached about by homeowners who want to update and renovate.

The second most popular renovation request I get is for the much less social but equally hardworking space—the bathroom. Bathrooms are highly specialized and personalized rooms, and no single approach or design works for everyone or every space. Whether it's a bustling family bathroom or a spa-inspired en suite oasis, the design is really dependent on who is using it. The planning, material, and fixture selections are made to reflect the unique needs of each situation.

Renovating a bathroom is a balancing act between making the space more useful and aesthetically appealing, while at the same time juggling an intricate system of pipes, wire, vents, and other structural elements. Add to that plumbers, electricians, carpenters, tile setters, cabinet makers, drywall installers, glass fitters—and maybe even a designer or two!—and you've got your hands full! Imagine all of them jammed into what is typically the smallest room in the house and you'll begin to understand the sheer complexity of renovating a bathroom. This also explains why inch-for-inch, bathrooms are typically the costliest remodels undertaken by homeowners. But sweet solace can be found in the fact that bathroom renovations rank at the top of the list in resale value, often recouping up to 90 percent of their cost.

Kitchens and bathrooms are the hardest-working rooms in house, without a doubt. And simply put, if they don't function well, *we* don't function well! Over the years and through the hundreds of kitchens and bathrooms that I've remodeled, I've learned that beautiful, functional, and creative design can bring harmony, organization, and comfort into any home and family. And that's something worth investing in!

Olson

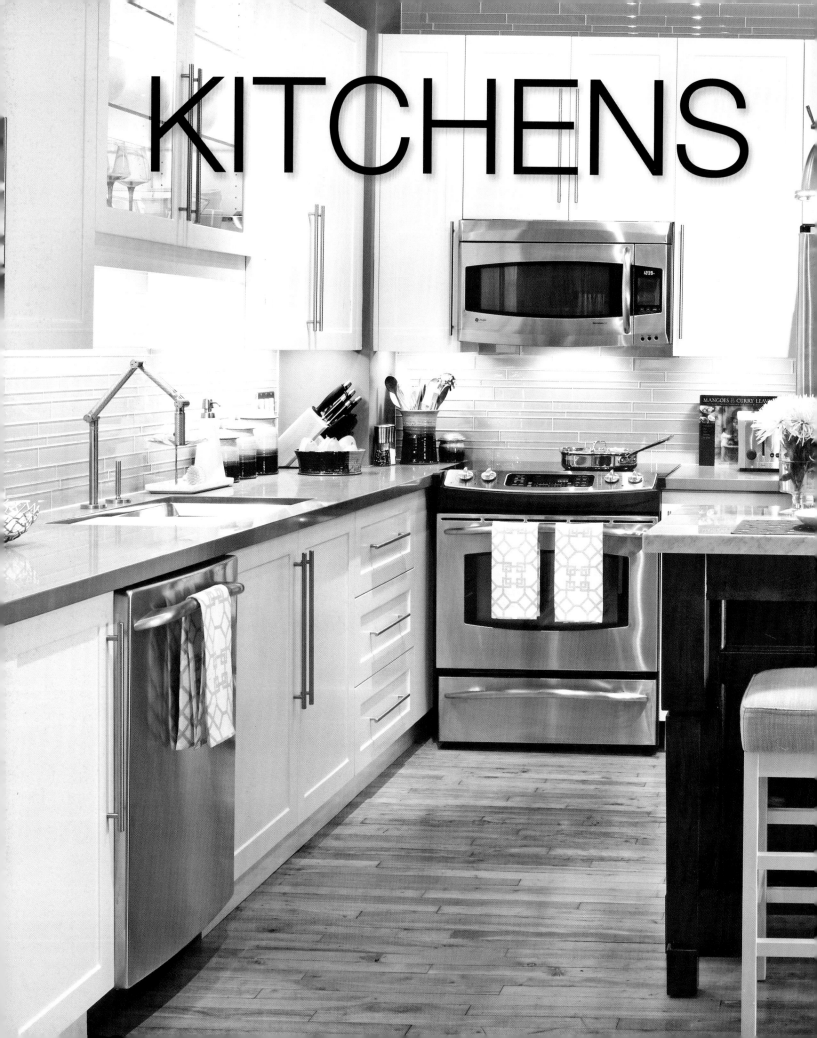

KITCHENS

Hostess Etiquette

1. DO NOT ORDER ONLINE.

2. KISS THE COOK!

3. PICK UP KIDS.

4. PICK UP HUSBAND.

5. CANCEL TAKE-OUT.

6. CELEBRATE !!

7.

1 FABULOUS FAMILY SPACES

TWO'S COMPANY, FIVE'S A CROWD

CHALLENGE

Where to begin? The large, L-shaped kitchen in this old farmhouse buzzed with activity; Deb and Greg's five teenage kids, their friends, and their friends' friends traipsed in and out all day long! Well-used and well-loved, the room had suffered a lot of wear and tear and was enormously inefficient. There were only two electrical outlets, so when Deb wanted to bake, she had to use extension cords. And although the island was big, it was far from functional and mostly served as a dumping ground for the kids' book bags. Annoyingly, when the dishwasher door was open, it blocked access to the cabinets. And Deb's view at the sink? A blank wall. The heart of this home needed major surgery to bring it back to life, stat!

BEFORE: With inadequate storage, poorly positioned work centers, worn-out cabinets, and a space-gobbling island that only served as a dumping ground for book bags, this kitchen couldn't keep up with the rigorous demands of a family of seven.

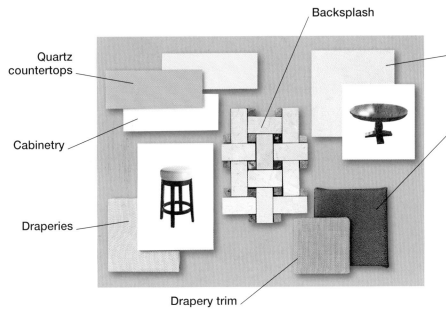

Backsplash

Quartz countertops

Leather for bar stools

Cabinetry

Chair seats, breakfast area

Draperies

Drapery trim

AFTER: A completely reconfigured space features more cabinets, a 60-inch-wide freezer-refrigerator (hidden behind cabinetry doors), stacked convection ovens, an under-counter microwave, and a built-in wine cooler. The function-packed island includes a sink, dishwasher, garbage bin, and eating area.

ABOVE: Cork floors are soft underfoot yet durable and easy to maintain. White leather upholstery on the bar stools is also easy to live with—just wipe it clean. The pantry tucked into the corner has pull-out shelves so Deb can see when she needs to re-stock on supplies.

SOLUTION

- The kitchen's floor space was fine, but the cabinets, appliances, and flooring were well past their best-by date, so it was out with the old and in with the new. Custom cabinetry with quiet, self-closing doors and drawers replaced all of the old cabinetry in the kitchen as well as a hutch in the dining area.

- Hardworking, family-friendly quartz countertops will stand up to lots of use from a herd of teens.

- I designed a new island loaded with function—a double sink, a dishwasher, and a pull-out garbage bin, plus seating for seven. The kids can grab breakfast or a snack, and the island provides spillover seating when there's a crowd. And one of the best features? Now Deb has a view of the beautiful outdoors when she's working over the sink.

- Deb spends a lot of time cooking and baking, so to give her a floor that would be comfortable and still be impervious to wear and tear, I chose cork. It's eco-friendly, soft underfoot, and self-healing—any small scratches or dents will seal back up over time.

- To make cooking faster and more efficient, I installed some terrific new appliances: double-decker convection ovens, a microwave, and a 36-inch induction cooktop. Induction technology is a perfect solution for Deb's short-order kitchen. The glassy surface stays cool to the touch until it comes in contact with stainless steel; then it heats quickly, cooking in a fraction of the time of conventional gas or electric cooktops. Remove the pan, and the surface is cool again. Brilliant!

- Feeding five hungry teens and their friends takes a lot of groceries, so I replaced the old refrigerator and freezer with a whopping 5-foot-wide unit, perfect for storing both fresh and frozen food. The grocery store clerks are going to miss seeing Deb and Greg!

- I added more electrical outlets to serve every work surface and even a large appliance garage to discreetly conceal Deb's many mixers and processors.

RIGHT: The backsplash ties the color scheme together with a basketweave pattern of marble and natural stone tiles in vanilla, mushroom, and espresso. Food cooks quickly on the induction cooktop, yet the heating elements stay cool to the touch.

STYLE ELEMENTS

- Deb and Greg wanted the new kitchen to have enough of a rustic, country feeling to blend with the rest of the house, yet still project a fresh, contemporary mood. I chose perimeter cabinetry with a traditional-style raised panel and selected a vanilla finish with a strié wash for an antique look. Matching doors for the refrigerator-freezer unit blend it into the cabinetry for a unified effect.

- For the new island, I chose espresso-color cabinetry with traditional turned legs to support the countertop extensions. The dark, rich color matches the chocolate hue of the cork floor and helps ground the space. Mixing light and dark cabinetry also helps keep the feeling casual.

- To keep tones in balance, I chose mushroom-color quartz for the perimeter counters and creamy quartz for the island. A backsplash of marble and natural stone tiles in a basketweave pattern ties the color scheme together. The polished finish ensures that the backsplash will be easy to clean, and the basketweave adds pattern in a room full of solid colors.

- Recessed ceiling fixtures around the perimeter of the room and fixtures under the cabinets give Deb plenty of good light for cooking. Pendants positioned about 16 inches apart over the island help break up the air space and illuminate the work/eat surface.

- Details help give the room a sense of history that is true to this old home. A burnished-bronze finish and vintage designs for the cabinet hardware, pendant fixtures, sink faucet, and chandelier in the dining area harken back to turn-of-the-twentieth-century kitchens and give this modern space a gently rustic feel.

LEFT: A deep double sink in the island allows Deb to enjoy the outdoor view while prepping or washing up. A gooseneck faucet in burnished bronze brings in a sense of history.

OPPOSITE: A new super-functional buffet in the dining area includes pull-out bins for files. The cream-color draperies look like silk but are actually easy-care polyester; the mushroom band on the leading edge won't show fingerprints.

THE HEART OF THE HOME

CHALLENGE

This very blue, 40-year-old kitchen was slated for renovation when Jeff and Chantal discovered that child #3 was on his way. But baby James came into the world with serious heart problems, and reno plans were put on hold while the couple focused on his care. Two years later, James and his brother and sister are healthy, happy bundles of energy, and Chantal feels like a short-order cook working in a too-small, dated kitchen. The painted cabinets are peeling, the doors won't close, and perhaps worst of all, the kitchen is cut off from the family room, preventing her from keeping an eye on the kids. Chantal and Jeff long for a space where the whole family can be together.

BEFORE: Forty-year-old cabinets, overbearing blue walls, and too little space made cooking in this dysfunctional kitchen a real challenge. A niche on the right (not seen) held a breakfast table for family meals.

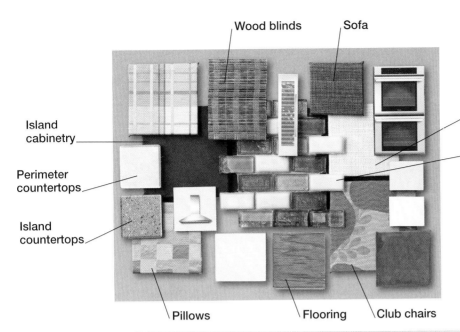

Wood blinds
Sofa
Island cabinetry
Perimeter countertops
Island countertops
Draperies
Backsplash
Pillows
Flooring
Club chairs

AFTER: Tearing down the wall that divided the kitchen from the family room opened a whole new world of family living and entertaining. A new, larger window above the sink overlooks the backyard so Chantal can keep an eye on the kids.

LEFT: The old eating niche is now a high-efficiency cooking center, with double wall ovens, a warming drawer, and an under-counter microwave. Beautiful glass tile mosaic on the backsplash brings together the colors of the woods and fabrics, accented with a lovely iridescent watery blue.

BELOW: A luxuriously large island with hefty turned legs provides visual separation between the two spaces and a spot for eating as well as work space. Dark walnut wood picks up the darkest tones in the oak floor and helps ground the space. Chalkboard paint turns a cabinet door into a message center.

SOLUTION

- Creating the open-plan concept that Chantal and Jeff wanted began with knocking down the wall between the cramped kitchen and the adjoining family room. I ditched all of the cabinets, flooring, and fixtures and had much larger openings cut for the sliding doors and kitchen window, to give clear views of the backyard and pool.

- To divide this big, open space into functional zones, I designed a gorgeous long island with counter space for eating as well as acres of room for food prep.

- The quirky little niche that had held the family breakfast table became the new cooking and fresh-food zone. Because Chantal is constantly cooking—often for a large crowd—I installed not one but two wall ovens with a warming drawer and an under-counter microwave. The refrigerator and freezer hide behind paneled doors, which won't show little fingerprints the way stainless steel would.

- Around the corner from the niche, the cooktop and range hood make a new focal point to anchor the view from the reconfigured family room. The cooktop is just steps from the sink, convenient for filling pots with water, and there's plenty of counter space on each side for food prep or resting hot pans.

- A huge, deep, cast-iron sink (big enough for washing the kids!) sits under the window, so Chantal can see the backyard while loading the dishwasher or washing vegetables.

- For the flooring, I chose a mid-tone oak with an antiqued texture that won't show wear from six little feet (and four big ones).

- Perimeter cabinetry includes loads of drawers for storage under the counter and a mix of closed and open shelving on the walls.

- Short-order cook Chantal needed restaurant-quality counters, so I chose über-durable quartz for the perimeter walls. It won't stain or scorch and stands up to hard use. For the island, I selected polished granite to pull together the creams and browns of the cabinetry and floor. Granite can take the heat as well, and although it needs periodic sealing to prevent stains, this mottled variety will disguise small accidents.

- The backsplash is like jewelry for the kitchen, and I wanted a lot of it— miles of tiles, in fact! I found a beautiful handcrafted glass tile mosaic that pulled together the colors of the woods, the fabrics, and the countertops and had a watery blue accent as well. This type of mosaic comes in squares glued to a paper front. After you attach the mosaic to a prepared wall, you sponge the paper off and then apply grout.

- Because the kids spend the summer splashing in the pool, the sliding glass doors are a super-high-traffic area. To protect the wood floors from wet feet, I stopped the wood about a foot from the doors and installed durable stone mosaic tile along the threshold.

STYLE ELEMENTS

- To make the new kitchen-family room truly feel like the heart of the home for this active young family, I wanted to create an eclectic look that would feel warm and relaxed, yet stand up to hard use. A mix of finishes says "eclectic"—painted perimeter cabinets in the kitchen, stained wood on the island and matching custom cabinets in the family room, and a medium-brown stain on the oak floor. Hardware mixes it up too, with traditional pulls in the family room and polished steel in the kitchen.

- For a light, airy look, I chose shades of creamy white for the walls, cabinets, and countertops. A strié finish on the cabinets ages them gently, and the mottled appearance of the quartz countertops gives a very soft effect.

- Contemporary bar chairs pick up the walnut color of the island but bring in a sleek, modern line that contrasts with the island's traditional turned legs and recessed-panel doors. Jeff especially wanted bar chairs with foot rests—and he got them!

- Vintage-style pendants over the island pair up with modern recessed lighting to give Chantal plenty of light to work by. One kid-friendly thing about the pendants—they're suspended on cables rather than rods, so they'll "give" if they happen to be bumped by a flying Nerf ball.

- Hard-wearing, kid-friendly fabrics upholster the new sectional sofa and chairs. I chose a dusty cocoa brown for the sofa—great for hiding dirty fingerprints—and a coordinating print for the club chairs. White linen curtains at the sliding glass doors blend with the walls, but the leading edges are banded in a darker fingerprint-hiding linen that relates to the finishes in the kitchen and family room.

LEFT: When the kitchen and family room are part of one large space, some of the kitchen functions might find their way into the family room. Here a wine fridge with a satellite bar sink can take on entertaining duties away from the hubbub of the kitchen.

OPPOSITE: In the family room, custom walnut cabinets bring the wood of the island into the family room and help set off the antique white kitchen cabinets. Comfy low-back chairs pair with the sectional sofa and don't interfere with sight lines to the television.

27

A cozy seating arrangement in the new family room opens to the kitchen, allowing Chantal to talk with her guests while she cooks. Soft faux-suede upholstery on the sofa has grownup good looks but is kid-proof and easy to clean. The extra-wide sliding doors give Jeff and Chantal a clear view of their beautiful backyard.

28

To Do:
(or not to do.)
- pick up kids
- cook
- drop off kids
- cook
- soccer game
- cook

TWO COOKS IN THE KITCHEN

CHALLENGE

Morning rush hour started for Harmeen at home before she even left the house! Her family faced a human traffic jam in their cramped, dysfunctional kitchen, causing fender-benders and pile-ups when mom Harmeen and her daughter, Niki, tried to cook while twin teen boys dodged between them. The refrigerator door blocked access to the breakfast table when opened, and the microwave was stuck back in the corner behind the table. There wasn't enough storage, and particularly frustrating were the spices—essential to the family's traditional Indian cooking—that were stacked six deep in the dated 1970s cabinets. This kitchen was fizzlin' when it should have been sizzlin'!

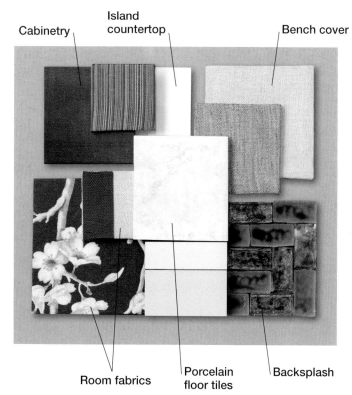

Cabinetry
Island countertop
Bench cover
Room fabrics
Porcelain floor tiles
Backsplash

BEFORE: The cramped work zone lay right in the path to the breakfast area. A compact space for one cook, the kitchen became a traffic hazard with two cooks and frequent snack hunters popping in.

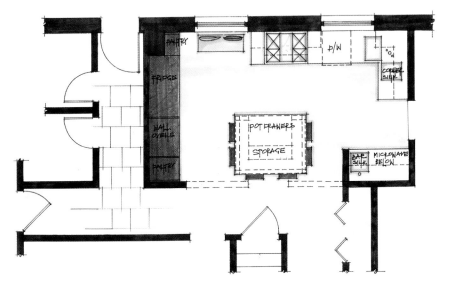

AFTER: Knocking out a nonload-bearing wall and designing a new configuration for cabinetry and appliances creates a tasty space for multiple cooks to create elaborate feasts.

ABOVE: Replacing the cramped U-shaped work zone with a long bank of cabinets and countertops makes room for a larger cooktop, complete with grill for cooking Indian specialties, and a large dishwasher.

SOLUTION

- Following my own not-so-secret recipe, I started with demolition. Tearing out a nonload-bearing wall opened up the kitchen and borrowed space from the adjacent hallway. We tossed all the old appliances, cabinets, counters, flooring, fixtures, and wallpaper to make way for a new, family-friendly kitchen.

- Breaking up those traffic snarls meant creating an open plan with easy access to appliances for one or more cooks. Along the outside wall where the old sink had been, I installed a long bank of cabinets with plenty of counter space for food prep on either side of the new gas cooktop. The cooktop includes a grill so Harmeen and Niki can whip up traditional Indian dishes year-round. Pull-out cabinets beside the cooktop put spices right where they're needed and keep them away from heat.

- Instead of a single large sink, I chose a double-basin sink that turns the corner, with a dishwasher on one side and prep space on the other (see page 34).

- I designed the nearby bar area with leaded-glass doors on the upper cabinets so it would look like a buffet beside the doorway to the dining room (see page 35). A small bar sink lets the boys get a glass of water without interfering with dinner preparations. The under-counter microwave is convenient for both cooks and snack-hunting teens.

- To give Harmeen more storage and cooking capacity, I designed a "wall of fame" along the entire back wall—two pantries, a 40-inch side-by-side refrigerator-freezer, two beautiful wall ovens, and a warming drawer. ("Mom, where's dinner?" "Look in the drawer!")

- Instead of a breakfast table in a dead-end space, the kitchen now boasts a show-stopping, custom-designed, focal-point island. The hardworking quartz top is big enough for food prep and dining. Self-closing drawers on one side of the island store flatware and dishes.

- Because one window was too deep for cabinets to be installed under it, I designed a bench with cookbook storage underneath. It sits in front of the window without blocking the light.

RIGHT: Column-style legs support the island counter extension on three sides, so contemporary bar chairs can slip underneath. On the fourth side, drawers provide much-needed storage for flatware and dishes.

STYLE ELEMENTS

- To create visual flow between the dining room and the kitchen, I picked a dark cherry finish for the cabinetry that brings in the color of the dining table and chairs. Traditional details—classic crown moldings, recessed panel doors and drawers, turned posts for the island legs, and leaded glass on the buffet—create a look of quality and elegance. Sleek hardware, stainless-steel appliances, and contemporary lighting add up to a yummy mix of styles that makes the kitchen sizzle!

- To balance all the dark vertical surfaces, I chose light, creamy colors for the horizontal ones. Mottled porcelain tiles on the floor give the look of limestone at a more affordable price, and white quartz countertops with teeny dark flecks tie into the dark cabinetry.

- With all of the solid-color surfaces, I needed to stir in a dash of pattern, so I selected handmade translucent and opaque glass tiles laid in a herringbone pattern for the backsplash. The 1×2-inch tiles have an iridescent quality when they catch the light, a bonus benefit of the task lighting mounted under the cabinets.

- Dark woven grass blinds at the windows match the cabinetry and become an extension of it.

- Because the island is the first thing you see when you come through the front door of the house, the chandelier over it needed to be a showpiece fixture. A gorgeous polished chrome and crystal fixture makes an architectural statement, with frosted bulbs to minimize glare and diffusers for shades. Recessed ceiling lights provide even lighting coverage throughout the kitchen.

OPPOSITE: The bar sink doubles as a second prep sink. The microwave is handy to the food-prep area but easy for the boys to use without getting in the way while Harmeen and Niki are cooking. A herringbone pattern of glass and opaque tiles on the backsplash reflects light and adds texture to the walls.

LEFT: For a kitchen with two cooks, two sinks are better than one! Sinks that turn the corner, with a shared gooseneck faucet and sprayer in between, free up prep space on either side.

FAMILY CENTRAL

CHALLENGE

This tiny kitchen was command central for super-chef Sue and her sous-chef partner, James. Sue and James love hosting family dinners and holiday gatherings, but it's been quite a challenge in these cramped quarters. Now, with in-laws and grandchildren expanding the head count, Sue and James wanted the kitchen of their dreams—roomier, with ample storage and top-of-the-line appliances to handle all the fabulous cooking they love to share.

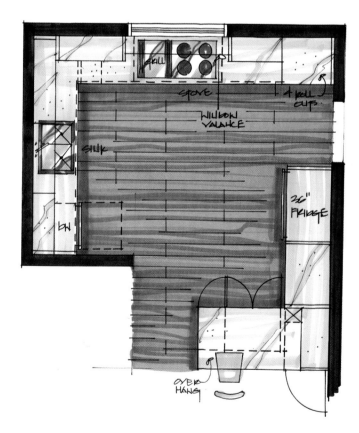

BEFORE: This modest kitchen seemed to shrink as James and Sue's family expanded, making cooking for the crowd increasingly difficult.

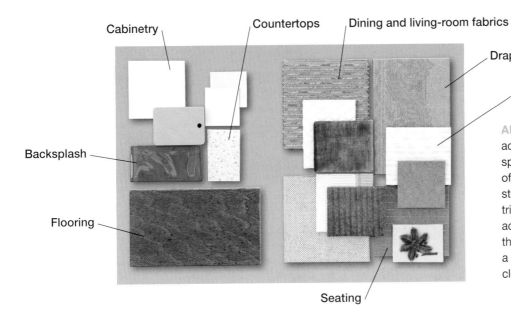

Cabinetry

Countertops

Dining and living-room fabrics

Drapery panels

Sheers

Backsplash

Flooring

Seating

AFTER: Opening the kitchen to the adjoining dining room creates more space for a bigger prep area, state-of-the-art appliances, and additional storage space. I reconfigured the work triangle completely to create better access for multiple people working in the kitchen. Vanilla-finish cabinets and a dark-brown tile backsplash balance a clean, bright feeling with cozy warmth.

SOLUTION

- To give Sue a kitchen that would match her culinary wizardry, I started by removing the wall separating it from the adjoining dining room. This creates a large, open-concept space that allows Sue to chat with guests while she's working in the kitchen.

- Gutting the kitchen top to bottom included eliminating a space-wasting bulkhead. This allowed for the installation of new cabinets that go right to the ceiling, adding more head space for storage. Storage options include a plate rack, stacks of drawers, and open shelving, giving Sue more flexibility to keep her cooking and food supplies right where she needs them.

- A long eating counter divides the kitchen from the dining area, offering family members a place to pull up a stool and help with the slicing and dicing. There's more practical storage underneath, and the countertop can serve as a buffet for large family gatherings.

- To ease Sue's job as top chef, I reclaimed the old breakfast area for double wall ovens—one of them a convection microwave—a warming drawer, and a huge new refrigerator (see page 40). Because she spends so much time at the stove, I installed the new state-of-the-art electric cooktop under the window so she can enjoy the view. There's a bonus oven to the right of the cooktop, which will help with major holiday feasts!

- A big new sink with built-in drainboard and cutting board and a pull-down spray head anchors the food-prep area. With a whisper-quiet dishwasher nearby, this corner is also an efficient cleanup center.

- Quartz countertops and a glass tile backsplash offer durability and easy care with the bonus of a fresh, up-to-date style.

- I updated the old parquet floor with new dark pre-finished hardwood flooring that visually weights the lightness of the cabinets. This type of wood flooring is not only quick and easy to install, but the factory finish is also tough as nails and a great choice for high-traffic kitchens.

OPPOSITE: This slick, all-electric cooktop includes an innovative built-in barbecue grill and a unique downdraft vent system.

LEFT: The new stainless-steel sink features a high gooseneck faucet with pull-out spray nozzle, ideal for filling big pots with water. The dishwasher is tucked into the corner, conveniently close to the sink.

STYLE ELEMENTS

- Warm vanilla cabinetry and countertops flecked with cream and brown brighten the space. The white finish helps maximize the natural light so that even with two smallish windows, the room doesn't feel dark.

- Dark-chocolate glass tiles pick up the brown flecks in the countertops and tie in visually with the new chocolate-finish floors. Laid in a stretcher bond pattern, the tiles resemble brickwork—a subtle reference to hearth and home for this family gathering place.

- Recessed ceiling fixtures around the perimeter of the room flood the cabinet faces with light, and under-cabinet lights brighten the countertops, giving Sue plenty of light to work by. Petite pendant lights over the peninsula help visually separate the kitchen and dining areas.

- The sparkling new kitchen raised the bar for the adjoining dining and living rooms, so I overhauled them as well! I continued the hardwood flooring into these spaces and repositioned the dining table so it can easily expand for a crowd. Comfy new chairs and beautiful new silk draperies infuse the dining area with relaxed elegance. Sue's favorite color scheme of Mediterranean blue, vanilla, and warm tan carries through the two rooms for a unified feeling.

ABOVE: Positioned parallel to the peninsula, the couple's original dining table easily expands to seat a crowd. New upholstered chairs reflect the new color scheme that carries into the living room.

BELOW: I'm smelling a family feast! A new professional-size refrigerator and commercial-quality ovens and warming drawer outfit Sue's new dream kitchen. The peninsula countertop extends out on the dining room side to accommodate bar chairs for kitchen helpers or extra diners.

UPDATED DINER

CHALLENGE

With its sea-foam blue cabinets, this outdated 1950s kitchen was a blast from the past—it made me want to put on my bobby socks and saddle shoes and get out my Hula-Hoop! Even though the countertops and appliances were newer, the kitchen still said retro, and not in a good way. It had lots of windows and great natural light, but the view of the neighbor's brick house was a little too close for comfort. Kelly and Rob have two young sons, and they wanted a contemporary and comfortable family-friendly kitchen where they could all be together—Mom and Dad cooking while the kids do homework and everyone enjoying dinner together.

BEFORE: A remnant of the fab fifties, this kitchen had seen its better days a half-century ago. The layout worked, but nothing else did—time for a modern renovation!

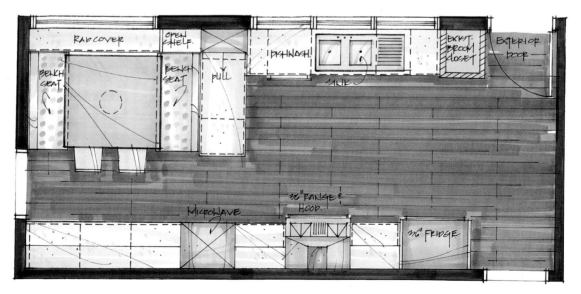

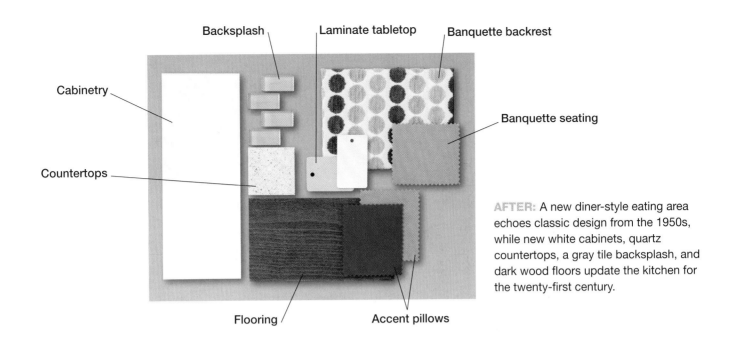

Cabinetry

Countertops

Backsplash

Laminate tabletop

Banquette backrest

Banquette seating

Flooring

Accent pillows

AFTER: A new diner-style eating area echoes classic design from the 1950s, while new white cabinets, quartz countertops, a gray tile backsplash, and dark wood floors update the kitchen for the twenty-first century.

SOLUTION

- Bringing this mid-last-century kitchen into the modern era meant starting from scratch, so I had all of the cabinets and counters, flooring, lighting, bulkhead, and appliances ripped out and hauled off. The small freezer and washer/dryer were moved to the basement to free up space for a much-needed larger refrigerator. This also opened up a clear path to the outside door.

- Under those passé cabinets and counters, the kitchen's bones were good, so I kept the basic layout. The idea of dividing the cooking and eating areas with a peninsula works as well now as it did in the past, and placing the sink under the windows with the dishwasher right beside it makes perfect sense. To bring in a new, classic look, I chose recessed-panel cabinetry for both the walls and the peninsula. The clean, white cabinets help brighten an already well-lit space. Cabinetry hardware mimics the atomic-age lines of the originals—some things never go out of style!

- To temper the brightness of the cabinets, I chose dark pre-finished hardwood floors. They're hard-wearing and stay beautiful in spite of spills and foot traffic. (They can even stand up to a sock hop!)

- The new eating area pays homage to the home's 1950s roots with a comfy dining banquette that's super-functional for family meals and homework. I enclosed the old radiator with a box and vent and designed banquette benches with cushioned backs to fit the new space. A turquoise laminate table with a pedestal base sits snugly in between. Burger and fries, anyone?

- For the backsplash, gorgeous glass tiles give the contemporary look Kelly and Rob want. To highlight the tile without creating a glare, I had the under-cabinet lighting installed close to the front of the cabinet. This way the countertop and backsplash will be evenly illuminated without any harsh reflections.

- My favorite countertop material is quartz, one of the hardest materials known to man and virtually maintenance free. As a bonus, some manufacturers infuse the material with an antibacterial agent, so it's a healthy choice as well as a practical one.

- High-functioning stainless-steel appliances make food prep a breeze. In addition to a large, quiet fridge, I installed a fabulous 5-foot-long sink with a cutting board surface and removable colander, which concentrates food cleaning and prepping in one convenient area. A high-performance gas range with a range hood, drop-down warming rack, and a combination convection and electric oven offer fast and efficient cooking for a busy family. The microwave oven, installed at waist height, looks built-in thanks to a clever trim kit. It's got 10 power levels and the all-important popcorn button!

STYLE ELEMENTS

- To balance the soft white cabinets and walls, I selected dark gray glass tiles for the backsplash—gray is chic and contemporary and picks up the color of the stainless steel. Black countertops would have looked elegant, but Kelly wanted to keep the kitchen light, so I opted for a light gray quartz with silvery flecks that tie into the stainless steel and the glass backsplash tiles.

- For some color and comfort, I chose turquoise washable faux suede for the comfy banquette cushions and a retro-inspired blue and sage chenille polka-dot fabric on the upholstered backrests. With the turquoise table, the fabrics and color scheme give a nod to the past but keep a fresh, modern edge.

- To give Kelly and Rob options—lots of options—for controlling light and views at the windows, I installed blinds that operate up or down from the middle of the window.

- A baker's dozen (plus) of recessed halogen fixtures lines the perimeter of the room to wash down on the cabinet faces. The old metal pendants that had hung over the peninsula had the right shape but were a little too big, so I replaced them with clear cylinders that illuminate the peninsula without blocking sight lines. A funky space-age fixture over the table adds fun style for dining.

BELOW: In the new configuration, a column of cabinetry breaks up the long expanse of countertop and provides the perfect spot for a new, easy-to-reach microwave oven. It looks built-in, thanks to a classy trim kit, but it's actually free-standing inside the cabinetry—making it easier to deal with when it needs replacing.

The original configuration, with the sink and dishwasher under the windows, worked well, so I kept the basic layout with the new cabinetry but brought in a 5-foot-long sink that has its own cutting board and colander. Blinds designed to raise or lower from the center allow more control over views and light.

PLAYDATE PARADISE

CHALLENGE

Looking at it with a "glass half full" attitude, Kurt and Lorraine's dated kitchen had one thing going for it—size. However, a poor layout meant this big kitchen ended up being just one big waste of space. An inefficient configuration and tiny windows made the room dark, dysfunctional, and cut off from both the sprawling backyard and adjoining main floor rooms. It needed a major "time out," if not outright reform school! Lorraine, a new mom, likes having neighborhood moms and their kids over for play dates and wanted a space that was stylish, kid-friendly, and inviting—a place where kids could play inside or out while under Mom's watchful eye.

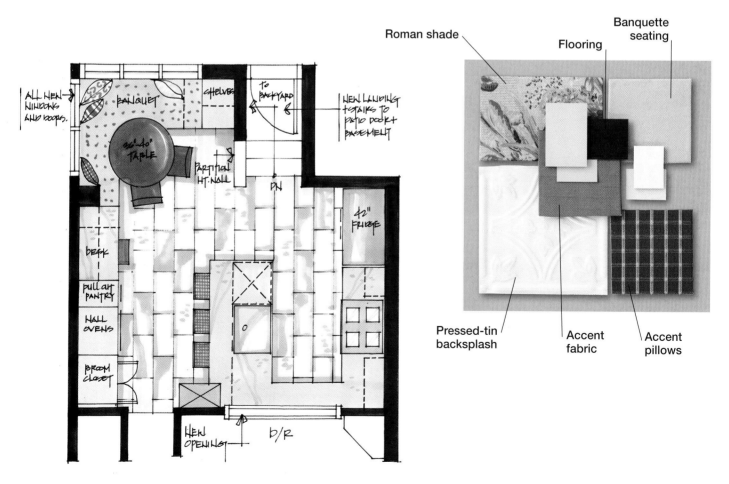

BEFORE: Wasted space and a bad layout meant lots of extra steps for Lorraine and Kurt, and the style was definitely dated.

AFTER: The completely reconfigured space now connects to the adjoining dining room through a new pass-through.

SOLUTION

- Envisioning a more practical, functional, and light-filled design, I opted to gut the entire kitchen—the floor, ceiling, cabinets, and a good portion of the back wall all had to go. The mudroom had been a major culprit in severing the kitchen from the backyard, so it got the ax, too. To allow the other main floor rooms to share the natural light and great view, I had a large opening cut for a pass-through between the kitchen and the dining room.

- New, larger windows wrap around the corner of the kitchen to create a sunny spot for a breakfast nook. The double-hung window is a nod to the traditional character of the home and adds a sense of history to this newly designed kitchen. The cozy banquette seating makes the most of an awkward basement staircase location by using the wall bump-out as a structural base for the seat cushions.

- One step down from the kitchen, a new landing leads to the back door for better access to the backyard. A window in the landing area lets even more light into the kitchen.

- To give Lorraine and Kurt a more functional area for food prep and cooking, I designed a step-saving U-shaped work space. A 42-inch-wide fridge and a cooktop with a chimney-style range hood line up along the back wall. The sink and dishwasher are within arm's reach on the other side of the U. Poured-in-place concrete countertops add an industrial touch that, combined with the modern stainless-steel appliances, brings a fresh contemporary attitude to this country-casual kitchen. The labor involved with poured and polished concrete counters often brings with it a premium price tag. However, my motto is if you can drive a car on it, you can cook and cut on it, making it the perfect hard-wearing choice for this busy family! All it needs is a regular sealing to maintain its rugged good looks.

- On the wall behind the counter stools, I kept the look streamlined with a built-in wall oven, warming drawer, and microwave, flanked by a pull-out pantry and broom closet (see pages 52–53).

- In the space between the pantry and the breakfast nook, I tucked in a small office area with a desk to help Kurt and Lorraine keep work-related clutter under control.

ABOVE: A sleek polished nickel faucet and poured-concrete countertops balance the traditional styling of the cabinetry. I like poured concrete for countertops because it's hard-wearing— if you can drive on it, you can chop on it!

OPPOSITE: A schoolhouse-style pendant lamp anchors the breakfast nook. It has the same vintage feeling as the double-lamp pendant over the sink (see page 49) but doesn't exactly match it. Light fixtures for different areas of the room don't have to match—they just need to get along!

STYLE ELEMENTS

- To make sure this space felt warm and sunny, I selected delicious shades of buttercream and vanilla for the walls. The same colors play out in the porcelain floor tiles and the cabinetry. To tie the kitchen visually to the adjoining living room, I had the ceiling painted in a lighter shade of the aqua on the living room walls. A similar color peeks out from the backs of the glass-fronted wall cabinets—a hint of indigo blue that creates flow between all the main rooms and adds a splash of cheery color to the neutral cabinetry.

- Kurt and Lorraine lean toward a carefree, country style—a look that's traditional but not formal or stuffy. Embossed tin ceiling tiles installed as a backsplash and painted to match the cabinetry help build that character. Other traditional elements, such as the inexpensive bead-board paneling on the front of the banquette and the recessed-panel style of the cabinets, are balanced by the contemporary elements of concrete and stainless steel to create a kitchen that is classic yet current.

- Recessed low-voltage ceiling lights around the perimeter of the kitchen are positioned to highlight cabinetry details and bring up the shine of sleek stainless-steel appliances. Lighting inside and under cabinets provides both accent lighting and lots of bright task lighting. For general ambient light I chose two vintage-style pendant fixtures, one over the eat-at counter and the other a schoolhouse style over the breakfast nook.

- Thick, comfy seat cushions covered in aqua faux suede top the banquette—soft to the touch and easy to clean. Roman shades in a vintage-inspired floral fabric bring together all the colors in the room and serve to accent rather than detract from the beautiful windows. With a conversation-inducing round table and a couple of chairs, this corner is ready for neighborhood moms and tots!

ABOVE: The built-in microwave, warming drawer, and oven fit in a neat, space-saving stack on the pantry wall. The sink peninsula is close at hand for resting baking dishes hot from the oven.

PANTRY WALL ELEVATION
1/2"=1'-0"

WEST ELEVATION

OPPOSITE: This compact office area gives Kurt and Lorraine a spot to pay bills and make up grocery lists. The stool tucks out of the way when the desk isn't in use, and it's easy to pull over to the breakfast nook if Lorraine needs extra seating.

COFFEE KLATCH KITCHEN

CHALLENGE

Every week the moms in my neighborhood get together in one of our homes for coffee, but every time it was Lisa's turn, I sensed her anxiety. Her 1960s kitchen was stuck in a definite time warp, with avocado-green cabinets and laminate countertops, fluorescent lighting, and ugly spaghetti-inspired acoustic ceiling tile. It would have been a big kitchen if there hadn't been a partial wall chopping it in half and blocking the view from one side to the other. Plus the windows were old, leaky, and wouldn't open. The moms voted her kitchen "Most Dated in the Neighborhood" and most in need of a marvelous modern makeover!

BEFORE: Stuck in the 1960s, this kitchen suffered not only from avocado-green cabinets and spaghetti-like acoustic ceiling tile, but also from an intrusive wall that chopped the room in half. Lisa had to bend over to peer through the opening and see her kids on the other side, and the kitchen half was pretty cramped when the moms gathered for coffee.

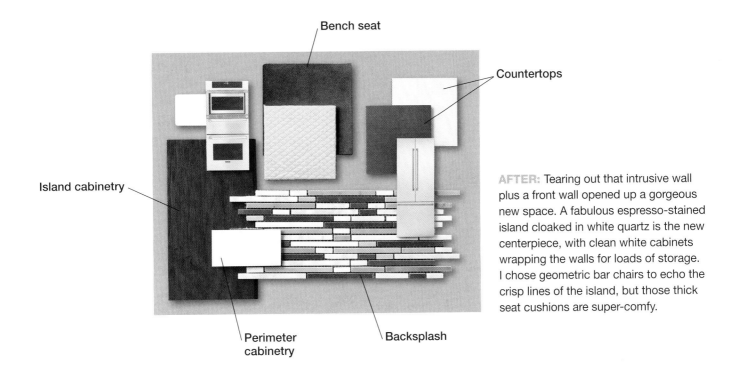

Bench seat

Countertops

Island cabinetry

Perimeter cabinetry

Backsplash

AFTER: Tearing out that intrusive wall plus a front wall opened up a gorgeous new space. A fabulous espresso-stained island cloaked in white quartz is the new centerpiece, with clean white cabinets wrapping the walls for loads of storage. I chose geometric bar chairs to echo the crisp lines of the island, but those thick seat cushions are super-comfy.

SOLUTION

- First I tore out a front wall that separated the kitchen from the hallway and living room and took down that awkward wall dividing the kitchen in half. All of the old cabinets and appliances were tossed as well, leaving a big, open-concept space ready for transformation.

- Because so much of the kitchen is about cabinetry, it's a good place to start in creating a new look. Classic recessed-panel, Shaker-style cabinetry with crown molding is both modern and timeless, and I lined Lisa's walls with tons of it to give her plenty of storage.

- I chose solid quartz for the countertops because it's durable and practically maintenance free. On the backsplash, a mosaic of thin marble strips adds character and spice.

- New hardwood flooring that comes in snap-together planks looks great and won't go out of style—and it's easy to maintain.

- New awning-style windows roll open to let in the air. This style of window gives you the largest expanse of glass possible without dividing the glass with mullions. The mullion detail on these windows and the sliding glass doors is actually a decorative band applied to the outside. I liked it because it's both traditional and contemporary—a win-win situation!

- A built-in bench under the side window offers another spot for sitting and talking. Drawers under the seat hide lots of stuff (we moms are messy!).

- For the room's focal point, I designed a luxuriously large island with seating for our gather-and-gab sessions. It also has an integrated electric cooktop with a pop-up range hood—just press a button and up comes the hood. Shazam!

- Double ovens with a warming drawer, a 36-inch stainless-steel refrigerator-freezer, and a super-tall beverage fridge with pull-out shelves and two cooling zones bring the kitchen's functionality into the twenty-first century.

OPPOSITE: I tucked a beverage center into one corner of the kitchen. The glass-front cabinet picks up on the glass door of the tall, skinny beverage fridge, which has pull-out shelves and two separate chilling zones. There's pop on top and wine below. What more could you ask?

LEFT: I used these ultra-cool leather and chrome handles and coordinating knobs throughout the kitchen for a sleek, modern look that reinforces the color scheme.

I call dibs on this spot for our next gathering at Lisa's! Dark charcoal velvet covers the plush seat cushion, and pillows in a range of grays play off the marble tile backsplash elsewhere.

Shaker-style cabinets combined with contemporary hardware and stainless-steel appliances create a look that's both modern and timeless. The double-door fridge has a bottom-mounted freezer—easier to get to the ice cream!

STYLE ELEMENTS

- A good way to create a modern look is to use a high-contrast color scheme. I chose crisp, fresh white for the walls and perimeter cabinets, with mahogany-finish floors and black quartz countertops. For the island, I reversed the formula—espresso-color stain with clean white quartz for the top and sides.

- The marble tile backsplash is the key component in this scheme, weaving the colors together—it's got the black of the countertops, the white of the cabinets, and a blue-gray that inspired the fabric colors for the window bench and draperies.

- One challenge with modern style is to keep it from feeling cold and sterile. That's where fabrics come in. I chose a luxurious charcoal velvet for the bench seat and blue-gray panels with grommets for the sliding glass door. The panels are designed to stack flat at the sides, clear of the doors, so they don't interfere with operation (see page 55).

- Unexpected traditional details like the twinkly crystal chandelier over the window bench also help soften modern design. Three mottled glass pendants with diffusers hang above the island to illuminate the cooking surface. They're a little bit modern and a little bit traditional, so you can't go wrong!

- Dark woven blinds hang at the windows to bring the color of the floor up the wall. Over the sink, the shade is mounted behind a cornice board, but above the window seat, the shade hangs at ceiling height to continue the line of the crown molding.

OPPOSITE: Diffusers shield the bulbs in these beautiful clear globes, eliminating glare.

ABOVE: Black and white are a culinary match made in heaven, with accents of cool gray and espresso brown to warm up the modern feel. The new stainless-steel sink includes a built-in cutting board for convenient food prep. New windows with integrated blinds can be cranked open to let in the air.

SMALL-SPACE SOLUTION

CHALLENGE

What you see on the Web isn't always what you get! Amanda and her family discovered this when they transferred back home from overseas and had to research and buy their house online. When they arrived with the moving van, they discovered that the "eat-in kitchen" was a tiny, narrow room with barely enough space for one person to work, much less room for their new baby's high chair! Amanda loves to entertain, and she missed the modern, open-space concept she'd had overseas. Plus, this kitchen was stodgy and boring, and she wanted an edgy, urban look that would still fit with the traditional architecture of the house.

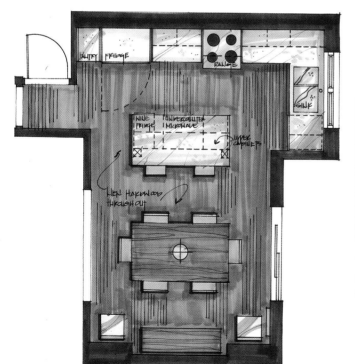

BEFORE: Tiny, tight, and tough to cook in, this kitchen felt cramped and chaotic. At night, the only illumination came from a line of track lights, so countertops were shrouded in shadow.

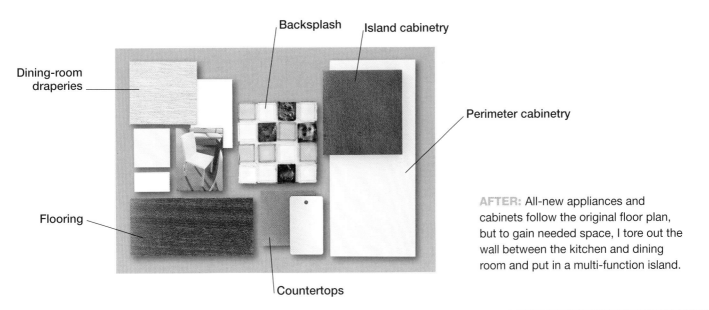

Dining-room draperies

Backsplash

Island cabinetry

Perimeter cabinetry

Flooring

Countertops

AFTER: All-new appliances and cabinets follow the original floor plan, but to gain needed space, I tore out the wall between the kitchen and dining room and put in a multi-function island.

SOLUTION

- Amanda's dream kitchen was only a sledgehammer away! Knocking out the wall that separates the kitchen and dining room is the number one way to turn a solo space into a social hub. It also creates the illusion of a bigger kitchen while staying within the existing footprint of the house. A new support beam keeps the second story in place.

- A gorgeous multifunctional island divides the dining area from the kitchen. On the kitchen side, the island provides much-needed counter space and houses the microwave and a wine cooler. On the dining room side, a raised counter and bar-chair seating invite friends to lounge while Amanda cooks.

- To bring in more light, I replaced the existing sink window with a much larger one and swapped the old swing-in French doors in the dining room for sliding glass doors. These energy-savers are double-paned, with maintenance-free aluminum frames on the exterior and style-friendly wood on the inside. The blinds are sandwiched between the glass so they never need dusting. Hooray!

- I replaced all of the old cabinets with recessed-panel cabinetry and installed them with composite quartz counters. This nonporous material is harder than stone, rendering it the number one choice when you want a countertop that resists scratching, scorching, and stains. Cabinets above the island have glass doors on both sides to allow light and views to pass through, adding to the feeling of openness.

- New pre-finished wood floors unify both spaces. The tough-as-nails factory finish made it the right choice for this high-traffic area, and the no-muss, no-fuss installation kept our labor costs down and our budget on track.

- To improve the kitchen's functionality, I installed a four-burner gas range with drop-down warming shelves, an ultra-quiet dishwasher next to the large, stainless-steel sink, and a stainless-steel fridge. I even tucked a DVD player and flat-screen TV into the corner, where Amanda can see it while cooking.

ABOVE: In the dining room, an attractive niche that had been hidden by a huge hutch now displays artwork and a custom-designed serving buffet. A mod-pod baby chair on a pedestal proves that children and contemporary style do mix!

OPPOSITE: A handsome, hardworking island is the centerpiece of the new space, with a microwave, a wine cooler, and prep counter on one side and a raised counter for eating and guests on the other. Gray drapery panels, stained wood trim, and hardwood floors tie the dining room to the kitchen visually.

STYLE ELEMENTS

- To blend Amanda's modern tastes with the traditional architecture of the house, I decided on an eclectic look that would merge the contrasting styles. Recessed-panel cabinets with crown molding address tradition, while sleek contemporary hardware, stainless-steel appliances, and composite quartz countertops that look like poured concrete bring in an edgy feel. Mixing painted and stained wood finishes suggests a kitchen that has evolved over time.

- For a fun color accent, I chose a backsplash of handcrafted glass mosaic tiles in shades of gray, dark blue, and vanilla. The scheme ties together the countertop, the cabinetry, and the colors in Amanda's dinnerware and accessories.

- Fabric helps the kitchen and dining room relate visually. Gray drapery panels over the patio doors speak to the soothing color of the countertops. And because the new patio doors have built-in shades for privacy and light control, the panels don't have to function. They can simply add softness and color (see page 65).

- Both areas needed help in the lighting department, so I had recessed ceiling lights installed down the center of the kitchen and around the perimeter of the dining room. Under-cabinet lighting brightens all of the work surfaces, and an inconspicuous clear glass bowl pendant illuminates the sink without blocking the view.

- In the dining room, a new, custom-designed table and easy-to-clean white leather chairs set the stage for entertaining. New sconces highlight the architectural niche and the new, streamlined buffet fits in comfortably. A square drum fixture over the table adds a contemporary flourish—and of course, the baby gets ultra-cool seating with a 1960s-inspired high chair!

BELOW: Just what every entertaining kitchen needs—a DVD player and drop-down TV tucked under the cabinet!

OPPOSITE: The new dishwasher is right next to the sink for no-drip loading. Big new windows allow in lots of light, and woven blinds provide a little privacy when necessary. The handcrafted-tile backsplash brings in the colors of the cabinetry, the countertops, and Amanda's accessories.

RIGHT: With the help of several coats of magnetic paint topped by chalkboard paint, a wall at one end of the kitchen becomes a message board. The words "Hostess Etiquette" and the numbered lines were applied with a graphic transfer—easier than hand-lettering them with paint!

A DOUBLE-DUTY KITCHEN

CHALLENGE

When I first saw this classic retro 1950s kitchen I thought of poodle skirts, homemade apple pie, and rock 'n' roll! And while I loved the retro authenticity, Peter and Kim were desperate for something more practical and modern. This kitchen is the hardest-working member of the family and has to serve double duty—not only do Peter and Kim cook family meals here, but they also test recipes for their gourmet specialty foods business. This family needed a functional, efficient space with plenty of room for both commercial food prep and everyday cooking—and that says new-millennium design to me!

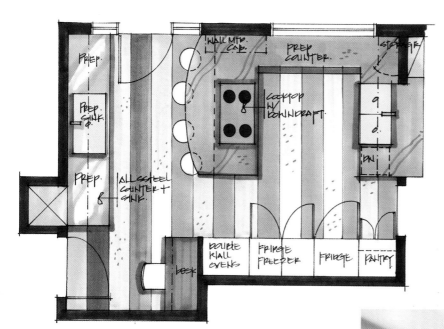

BEFORE: The eat-in kitchen in this ranch house hadn't seen an update since it was built in the 1950s.

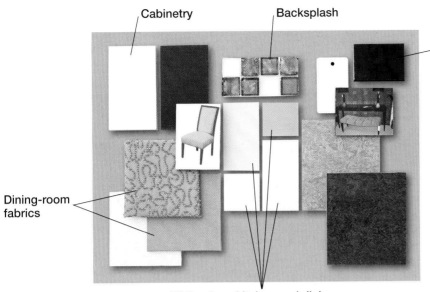

Cabinetry

Backsplash

Quartz countertops

Dining-room fabrics

Wall colors, kitchen and dining room

AFTER: I kept the big window for its great view of the backyard but pulled down the wall between the dining room and kitchen for a roomy, open-concept plan. The old eating area became the new, super-efficient space for cooking for friends and family.

SOLUTION

- The first thing to go was the wall between the kitchen and dining room. I decided to tear it out in order to create one large, open space. A bulkhead and partial wall give the dining room a little bit of enclosure without blocking the visual flow.

- For family meal prep, I laid out a U-shaped kitchen next to the dining area. With the sink on one side and the integrated cooktop in the opposite peninsula, there's plenty of counter space under the window for whipping up great meals for family and friends—and we know this family knows how to cook!

- Since Peter and Kim have more than the usual amount of groceries to store, I installed two refrigerators and loads of pantry space on the wall opposite the window (see page 74). Fridge door panels that match the cabinetry provide a sleek and seamless look. State-of-the-art double ovens opposite the peninsula can work for both the family area and the recipe-testing end of the kitchen.

- To handle the gourmet food testing, I designed a furniture-style unit for the back wall. The unit's dark wood, leaded-glass doors, and glass-tile mosaic backsplash make a gorgeous focal point from the dining room, but up close you can see it's a hardworking area, with a second oven, stainless-steel countertop, and a large stainless-steel sink with integrated drainboard.

- A small desk area rounds out the professional end of the kitchen, and a custom-built wooden wall unit provides open storage for Peter and Kim's collection of colorful cookbooks (see page 72).

LEFT: The integrated cooktop is so sleek you hardly notice it when it's not in use—and when it is, an automatic pop-up venting system whisks away smoke and cooking odors.

ABOVE: Beautiful recessed-panel cabinet doors hide the dishwasher, pull-out recycling and trash bins, and storage. I like dark brown woven blinds for a kitchen like this because they provide light control and privacy when you need them and a tailored valance effect when you don't.

STYLE ELEMENTS

- For a hardworking surface underfoot, I put down resilient flooring in light and dark gray stripes. This is an industrial product that resembles concrete and is often used in car showrooms and airplane hangars! It's a great flooring surface that's both durable and comfortable—an important combo for this much-used kitchen.

- To give the kitchen a fresh, modern look that would blend with the rest of the house, I chose traditional, recessed-panel cabinetry in crisp, white for the family area. Sleek polished chrome handles add a clean-lined, functional accent.

- To balance the traditional cabinetry, I chose black quartz countertops, which have a modern feel, and designed a random graphic pattern for the glass-tile mosaic and backsplash. Plastic-and-metal bar chairs tip the scales toward an overall comfortable contemporary look.

- For a quiet background that lets the cabinetry pop, I chose two shades of blue for the walls. With all the white cabinets and black countertops, blue is calming in the kitchen and elegant in the dining area.

- Good lighting is key to good kitchen design. Recessed ceiling fixtures around the perimeter of the room and under-cabinet lights banish irritating shadows and illuminate the work surfaces. And what's a room without a chandelier? A small crystal one over the family prep counter sparkles with a touch of glamour.

- To bring the dining room in line with the beautiful new kitchen, I kept the couple's table and brought in new upholstered dining chairs, new draperies, a chandelier, and fresh color on the walls.

ABOVE: I tucked a desk with wall storage into the corner near the recipe-testing center. It's perfect for making notes on testing results and planning the next product.

ABOVE: To display the couple's cookbooks and keep them handy, I designed this neat custom-built wooden bookrack for the office nook. It's only a few inches deep so it doesn't interfere with the door.

ABOVE: A classically styled mahogany unit with leaded-glass doors looks like an elegant piece of furniture at the back of the kitchen, but it's the testing and prep center for Peter and Kim's gourmet food business.

ABOVE: Hiding the refrigerators and pantry behind cabinetry panels gives this super-functional kitchen a warm, furnished look. Cookie sheets are stashed in the cabinet above the ovens.

OPPOSITE: New upholstered chairs surround the couple's original table to freshen the look. The partial wall separating the kitchen from the dining area includes a handy wine rack.

2 DESIGNED FOR ENTERTAINING

MID-CENTURY MAKEOVER

CHALLENGE

When they first purchased the house, this 1960s kitchen—complete with original copper-toned appliances—delighted husband Terry, a big fan of ranch-style architecture and sixties design. However, his wife Tracey wasn't so thrilled. Vintage appliances aside, they loved to entertain but the oh-so-typical isolated kitchen made it difficult to do. After five years of working in the cramped, out-of-the-way space and preparing meals with appliances almost a half-century old, Tracey finally got Terry to admit that it was time for a complete overhaul. My challenge was to design a modern kitchen/dining area that's perfect for entertaining while paying homage to Terry's love of mid-century design.

BEFORE: The swinging sixties lived on in this kitchen. With blonde cabinets and copper-toned countertops, appliances, and hardware, it was like a time capsule of mid-century modern style.

AFTER: The new kitchen is totally zen, sleek, and minimalist, but with long, low horizontal lines that pay homage to the home's ranch-style architecture. Slinky bar stools cozy up to the island's quartz countertop so guests can chat with the cook.

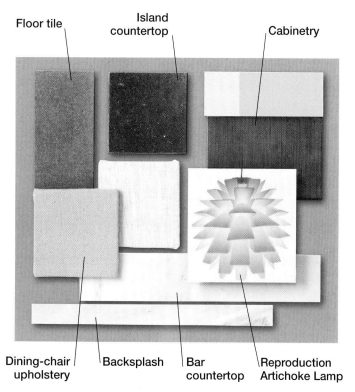

Floor tile

Island countertop

Cabinetry

Dining-chair upholstery

Backsplash

Bar countertop

Reproduction Artichoke Lamp

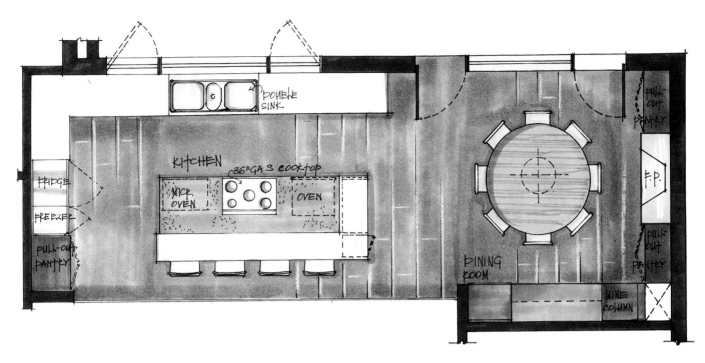

Labels in floor plan:
DOUBLE SINK
KITCHEN
36" GAS COOKTOP
MICR. OVEN
OVEN
FRIDGE
FREEZER
PULL-OUT PANTRY
PULL-OUT PANTRY
F.P.
DINING ROOM
PULL-OUT PANTRY
WINE COLUMN

SOLUTION

- We said goodbye to the copper appliances, vintage cabinets, and outdated flooring. The next thing to go was the wall separating the kitchen from the dining room, and I have to admit, this is where the scope of the project started to grow a bit. Terry and Tracey liked the openness so much that I proposed knocking down the dividing wall at the living room as well, creating one large open-concept kitchen, dining, and living room perfect for socializing with friends and family. This renovation would completely transform how this family lived in their home!

- New, larger windows and glass doors flood the entire area with natural light and visually and physically connect the space with the beautiful backyard patio—an area perfect for outdoor grilling and al fresco dining.

- To create visual flow, I picked up on the tone of the outdoor patio stones and brought that into the kitchen and dining area with slate-gray porcelain. The scale of the large-format tile relates directly to the large area to be covered—a smaller size would look too busy. This tile was the perfect companion for the medium-brown oak flooring that I chose for the living room, picking up on the darkest color within the wood grain.

- With most of the walls gone or converted to large windows or glass doors, there was little wall space left for upper cabinets, so I needed to plan for maximum efficiency. I started with the long quartz countertop that stretches the length of the exterior wall. The fridge, freezer, and large pull-out pantry occupy the only wall in the space—the short leg of the L—while the majority of storage is housed under the countertop in large pull-out drawers that utilize every inch of space. Seasonal or occasional-need storage is provided for in the dining room, either at table-side or discreetly hidden behind wall panels that flank the new fireplace.

- To handle food prep and cooking and provide plenty of space for casual meals, I designed a large, two-tiered island—big enough to qualify as its own continent! At the food-prep side, a sleek cooktop integrates seamlessly into the black marble countertop. Completely hidden from guests, an oven and microwave are positioned under the counter, keeping the look clean and uncluttered. To act as a visual barrier between the open-concept kitchen and living/dining room, a 42-inch-high, white quartz perimeter countertop embraces the cooking area in an L shape that mirrors the kitchen layout. This counter also provides a place for casual meals and entertaining.

ABOVE: Pantry storage with glide-out drawers and shelves that reach to the ceiling eliminates the need for upper cabinets along the adjacent window wall.

- On the dining room wall, I designed a counter and cabinetry configuration that functions as a table-side bar and buffet (see page 82). A state-of-the-art wine fridge and built-in coffee maker flank the buffet to frame and define the area. The black marble countertop is perfect for hot dishes, and the mirrored backsplash reflects the outdoors, giving the family and guests a view of the garden no matter where they're seated.

- At the dining room end of the room, I had an elevated gas fireplace installed at the height of the table so it can be enjoyed from all areas of the new space (see page 83).

ABOVE: Appliances stay out of sight with the fridge and freezer hidden behind zebrawood panels at one end of the kitchen and double ovens, microwave, and dishwasher tucked under counters or into the island.

STYLE ELEMENTS

- Throughout the kitchen, I wanted to pay homage to the long, low lines of mid-century modern architecture. I chose a high-contrast color scheme of white countertops and chocolate cabinetry, and it's the contrast between these major elements that helps emphasize the horizontal nature of the design.

- Long, open shelves repeat the horizontal movement, as does the grain of the zebrawood cabinets, which I chose to run horizontally rather than the more typical vertical fabrication. Both tiers of the quartz island countertop have a seamless waterfall return to the floor, creating a minimalist line (see page 79). This detail not only adds a beautiful sculptural quality to the island but also supports the countertop.

- The slab-front cabinet doors have the same clean look as the original 1960s cabinets, but the dark wood, accented with long chrome pulls, makes a more sophisticated, contemporary statement.

- Hiding the fridge and freezer behind cabinet doors allows the end wall of the kitchen to present a unified front, blending in with the rest of the cabinetry.

- I kept Tracey and Terry's existing dining room table but added new dining room chairs upholstered in a cream-colored fabric to provide contrast to the darker wood tones in this area.

- Five retro-style bubble pendants provide intimate dropped lighting and create a rhythm along the length of the island to help break up the expanse of countertop (see page 81). For the dining room, I chose a reproduction of the iconic 1958 Artichoke lamp originally designed by Poul Henningsen. It's an inexpensive salute to mid-century modern design.

- Tailored Roman shades mounted above the windows extend the height of the windows visually and leave the view open to enjoy. The dark woven grass repeats the color of the cabinetry at the ceiling line. Like the wall shelves, they reinforce the minimalist feel of the new space.

OPPOSITE: The bar area includes a wine refrigerator, built-in coffee maker, and storage for glassware, china, and table linens.

ABOVE: With clear sightlines in mind, I had the new fireplace installed above the height of the table. This way, it can be enjoyed from the kitchen, the island bar, or even from the new open-concept living room. Floor-to-ceiling cabinets on either side provide plenty of storage, complementing the abundance of space-maximizing, under-counter storage drawers in the kitchen.

ELEGANTLY UPDATED
FOR TWO

CHALLENGE

After years of long commutes, suburbanites Ken and Annette decided to move to the city. They found a charming Victorian row house within walking distance of their offices, but it needed loads of work, starting with the kitchen. "Updated" and enlarged at some point in the home's history, the kitchen was now a nightmare, with cracked laminate, peeling linoleum floors, and cabinet doors that wouldn't close. A dropped redwood ceiling made the kitchen feel cramped, while the breakfast area seemed unfinished and nonfunctional. My challenge was to combine Ken's desire for a sophisticated, über-modern look and Annette's wish to respect the architecture of the house by keeping in some traditional elements.

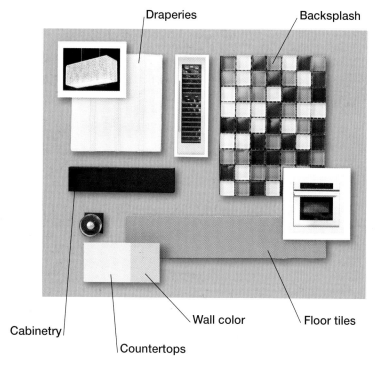

Draperies
Backsplash
Cabinetry
Countertops
Wall color
Floor tiles

BEFORE: Cracking laminate, peeling linoleum, and cabinets that wouldn't close stamped this kitchen as dated, worn out, and crying for help. The whole house, a heritage Victorian, needed renovating, but this was the place to start.

AFTER: One long wall of cabinetry and appliances, paralleled by a 14-foot-long island, transforms the kitchen into a sophisticated blend of high-style modern and elegant traditional. Espresso-brown, slab-front cabinetry is unmistakably contemporary, while crown molding and stunning crystal chandeliers speak to tradition. Note the runway lights down the back of the island to illuminate the porcelain-tile floor at night!

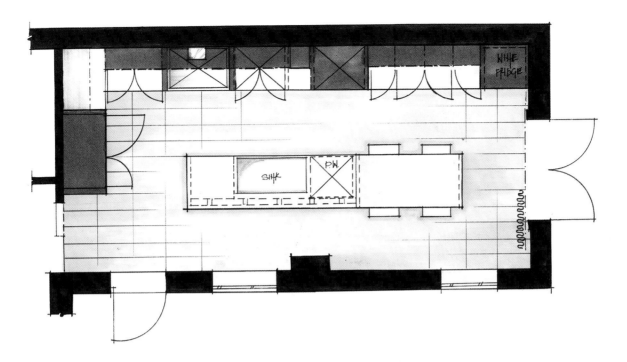

SOLUTION

- Nothing in this kitchen was worth keeping, so I stripped it back to the studs, tore out the dropped ceiling section, and ripped up the old floor.

- A new porcelain-tile floor laid over a radiant-heat pad is hard-wearing and will keep toes nice and warm in winter.

- An island was high on this couple's wish list, so I designed a fantastically long island—14 elegant feet! To keep it from seeming *too* long, I used a change in elevation to define two different zones: a 42-inch-high, bar-height counter that anchors the gathering area for the entertaining Ken and Annette love to do, and a standard-height, 36-inch-high counter for the food-prep area. This part of the island includes an oversized sink, dishwasher, and storage.

- For maximum step-saving convenience, I grouped the cooking functions on the perimeter wall across from the sink. To keep the look of the counters very clean-lined and uniform, I opted for a five-burner gas cooktop with a convection oven tucked discreetly under the counter. To further define the transition from kitchen to entertainment zone, I stacked the microwave, warming drawer, and espresso maker in a single, ultra-functional column at the end of the cooking area.

- At the gathering end of the island, I installed glass-front cabinets for glassware and a spacious serving counter for setting out appetizers and drinks. A beautiful two-zone wine refrigerator anchors the end of the cabinetry wall. Cheers!

LEFT: Open shelves on the end wall beside the freezer-fridge glimmer in the light of vertical accent lighting beside the cabinet. For the cabinetry hardware I chose crystal pulls and rods, combining a traditional material with sleek, contemporary shapes.

OPPOSITE: The 42-inch-high quartz-slab table at the end of the island is more social than a standard table height because people can stand, lean, or sit and be comfortable. The server space along the wall is ideal for setting out appetizers, food, or drinks.

ABOVE: A traditional damask pattern, enlarged and transferred to chocolate metallic vinyl, makes a dramatic accent on the wall and ceiling and pays homage to the home's historic roots. The large windows in this part of the house are obviously not original—and also not the same height. To disguise the different heights, I hung woven wood blinds at the same height on both walls.

STYLE ELEMENTS

- Cabinets have the most impact on style, and slab-front maple cabinets in an espresso finish say "modern" loud and clear. But wood is a traditional material, and the crown molding along the top discreetly whispers "traditional" as well.

- Quartz countertops in the purest white available set up a high-contrast dialogue with the cabinets to drive home the modern theme. Delicate glass-tile mosaic on the backsplash marries the two by picking up the dark and light tones and mixing in a third, middle tone that inspired the colors for the walls and floor.

- For a dramatic accent that would nod to the home's traditional style, I had an overscale damask pattern created on chocolate metallic vinyl. Transferred (with lots of firm burnishing) onto the wall and ceiling, it says traditional, modern, and whimsical all at the same time. It's multilingual!

- The room's windows and doors were of different heights, so to even them out I hung woven-wood blinds at the same level throughout the room. Sheer white draperies lined with dim-out fabric frame the patio doors. The fabric adds some softness to the room, and the draperies can be drawn for privacy without blocking access to the doors.

- Layers of light make this once-downtrodden kitchen really sparkle. Recessed ceiling fixtures, under-cabinet task lighting, vertical accent lights, and runway lights along the outside of the island ensure plenty of light for cooking and entertaining. For some show-stopping bling, I hung two crystal-bead chandeliers over the island. The crystals are a traditional material (for Annette), but the linear shape is totally modern (for Ken).

RIGHT: The sleek stainless-steel range hood is expandable—the filter tray slides out to extend over the front burners when Ken and Annette are cooking and slides back in line with the cabinets when they're not. On the backsplash, beautiful glass tiles in a mosaic of espresso, mushroom, and white pull the room's color scheme together.

HOLLYWOOD GLAMOUR

CHALLENGE

As a successful movie producer, Aubie is accustomed to a life of glitz and glamour. But the kitchen in his new home was awkward, outdated, and in need of a total overhaul to get the rave reviews it deserved! A dead-end breakfast nook and zigzag corners made this space a flop. Aubie loves old-style, 1920s Hollywood design and wanted a space to entertain large crowds in a kitchen that was worthy of critical acclaim!

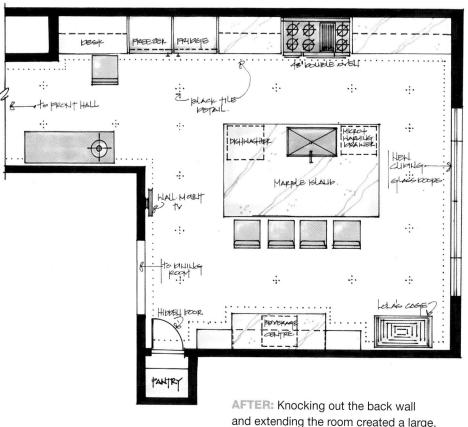

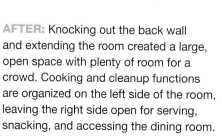

AFTER: Knocking out the back wall and extending the room created a large, open space with plenty of room for a crowd. Cooking and cleanup functions are organized on the left side of the room, leaving the right side open for serving, snacking, and accessing the dining room.

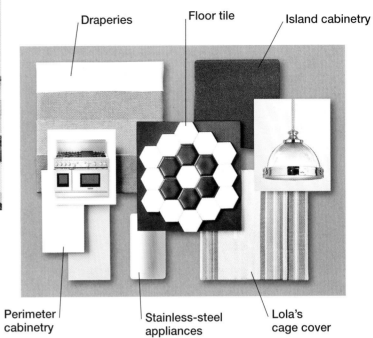

Draperies

Floor tile

Island cabinetry

Perimeter cabinetry

Stainless-steel appliances

Lola's cage cover

BEFORE: The old kitchen zigzagged its way to a breakfast-nook add-on at the back, passing another jog to the right for access to the back door. It was a poor layout for entertaining.

SOLUTION

- Aubie's glamorous guests needed more elbow room in this space, and that topped the list of requirements. I doubled the floor space by knocking out the wall where the kitchen window used to be, as well as the dead-end breakfast nook. Now the kitchen is one big room with sliding glass doors flanked by tall, multipane windows overlooking the backyard. The new room also connects to the adjoining dining space for a more even flow.

- Before laying the new tile floor, I installed a radiant heating system to keep the floor toasty in winter. Small white hexagonal tiles with a black-tile detail harken back to a classic 1920s look, and the black-and-white color scheme is a nod to Aubie's favorite black-and-white movies.

- Nothing in this space is understated! To handle cooking for a crowd, I put a gigantic double oven and a big stainless-steel fridge and freezer along one wall. A huge, gorgeous island in the middle of the room includes a microwave and warming drawer as well as the sink and dishwasher along one side. On the other side, bar stools tuck under the extended marble top so Aubie's friends can cozy up to the counter and enjoy cocktails while he cooks.

- On the wall opposite the cooking zone, I installed a pantry and beverage center with a mirrored backsplash. The beverage center is perfect for serving food and drinks. There's also a spot for Aubie's real "star"—his pet parrot Lola and her capacious cage.

ABOVE: On the guest-seating side of the island, cabinet doors conceal storage for seasonal items. The bar chairs make a modern statement but blend with the traditional elements through wood color and metal surfaces.

ABOVE: A custom covering for Lola's cage helps her—and Aubie—sleep later on Saturday mornings!

ABOVE: The pantry and beverage center is designed to look like a freestanding hutch—but with the modern touch of a built-in beverage refrigerator! Glass doors on the upper cabinets reveal the dramatic, black-painted interior, highlighted with in-cabinet spots. Lola's cage tucks into the corner, where from her perch she can while away afternoons gazing at the outdoors.

STYLE ELEMENTS

- The movie-inspired, black-and-white color scheme starts with the floor tiles and carries through the room with white subway tiles on the backsplash, white perimeter cabinetry, and the ebony-stained island and desk chair. I kept the contrast from feeling stark by painting the walls a warm neutral color and choosing a drapery fabric with a simple block design of cream, tan, brown, gray, and black.

- To anchor the room in traditional 1920s style, I chose simple, recessed-panel cabinets with crown molding and designed a turned, furniture-style leg for the island. An 8×5-foot honed marble top adds an old-world European feel. Large-scale pendants over the island provide ambient light with vintage style.

- Modern accents—the sleek kitchen faucet and under-mounted stainless-steel sink and those slinky modern bar chairs—balance the traditional look and add a bit of glamour.

- Nothing but the best for the leading lady! A custom-designed slipcover for Lola's cage helps her (and Aubie) catch more beauty sleep on sunny mornings.

ABOVE: This nifty stainless-steel under-mounted sink includes a cutting board and disposal, so Aubie can wash vegetables, prep, and scrape the peelings into the disposal—convenience at its best! The cooktop handles a wok and has a built-in griddle.

ABOVE: A sliver of space beside the fridge accommodates a built-in desk and wall cabinets—just enough office space to help Aubie organize his plans for entertaining.

ABOVE: The side-by-side refrigerator-freezer anchors one end of the cooking zone.

LIVE, WORK, EAT!

CHALLENGE

This teeny, tiny, totally outdated kitchen didn't work at all for Cal, a hip young animation artist and director. In fact, the whole first floor was a problem. This is his first home as well as his office, and as his career takes off, he needs a place that projects a professional image and provides comfortable space for brainstorming, creating animations, and meeting with musicians, artists, and clients. He also likes to cook for his friends, and that just wasn't going to happen in this shoebox of a kitchen. Clearly, this was a job for . . . Super Designer!

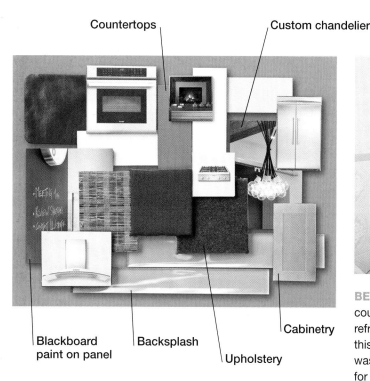

Countertops · Custom chandelier · Blackboard paint on panel · Backsplash · Upholstery · Cabinetry

BEFORE: This kitchen was unbelievably small, with no counter space, inadequate storage space, and a hard-to-reach refrigerator stuck back in a little nook (which you can't see in this photo). It was totally outdated, and the whole first floor was too compartmentalized to work well as a live/work space for a hip young animation artist.

AFTER: Knocking out all the interior walls created a loftlike open space with zones for a kitchen, office, and lounge. A table attached to the back of the island doubles as a dining table and work space. A custom light fixture overhead combines bare bulbs and cable in a bouquet of bright ideas.

SOLUTION

- Wearing my superhero cape, I knocked out all of the interior walls on the first floor to create one big open space. To keep the second floor from becoming part of the first floor, I installed support posts and beams where the load-bearing walls had been. Made of compressed and glued wood, they're stained for a warm, rustic feel, but I left the steel joinery exposed to create the look of a raw, industrial space (see page 100).

- The new kitchen occupies the same corner of the house as the old one did, but now it's part of an open-concept space that makes it feel roomier. A long counter with a sink, dishwasher, and built-in fridge fills one wall, and a super-functional island with a cooktop and range hood gives Cal the Master Chef plenty of elbow room for cooking.

- For cabinetry, I selected Shaker-style cabinets with recessed-panel doors. You can't go wrong with this style — it's clean-lined for a modern look, but has a hint of traditional character that grounds it as a classic.

- Stainless-steel appliances, including a 36-inch fridge with French doors, carry through the industrial look and upgrade the kitchen with function and style.

- To play up the backsplash as a focal point, I opted for linear strips of glass tiles in three widths and had them installed in a random pattern, similar to floorboards.

- Because the dining room is also Cal's boardroom, I attached a big table to the other side of the island, to double as dining and working space. To round out the office area, I designed two sleek quartz desks for the opposite wall. They're 30 inches high — just right for working at the computer — but in a pinch they can also serve as satellite cooking space.

- In keeping with the industrial-loft look, I chose oak plank flooring with a reclaimed, salvaged finish.

- Since this is a place where ideas are born, I had two huge blackboards installed, mounting one on a sliding-door mechanism to hide the pantry. Just the spot for working out a new story line — maybe about a superhero renovator-to-the-rescue? (I look pretty good in a cape!)

Cal Brunker

LEFT: Inspiration strikes! Cal's new idea: "Super-Renovator to the Rescue!"

ABOVE: To give the new space an industrial feel, I chose polished gray quartz for the island and countertops, a sleek, modern stainless-steel-and-glass range hood, and stainless-steel appliances. Glass tiles laid in a random pattern above the sink turn the wall into a focal point.

One big fabulous space easily hosts brainstorming meetings, interviews with clients, and parties with friends. Charcoal-gray felted upholstery fabric mimics luscious mohair, a luxurious contrast to rustic post-and-beam supports that replace a load-bearing wall. Floor-to-ceiling blackboard panels front a storage column beside the desks and slide aside to conceal pantry storage in the kitchen—perfect for chalking up a new cartoon series!

- Meeting 1pm
- Review Sketches
- Contact Illustrator

ABOVE: Along the wall behind the dining/work table, I placed two heavy-duty quartz desks and super-comfortable, ergonomic desk chairs. The raw linen draperies are backed with dim-out lining to protect the natural fabric from the sun and diffuse light, preventing glare on the monitors.

STYLE ELEMENTS

- Turning this open space into a fantastic, stylish idea factory that was also a comfortable place for relaxing and entertaining hinged on playing raw elements against refined ones. Indestructible quartz countertops resemble humble concrete, but polishing the quartz gives it a sense of refinement. The polished glass backsplash contrasts with the rustic finishes of post and beam, and natural linen curtains have a glazed finish that adds a little sheen.

- Warm, earthy neutrals give Cal's new space a hip, ultra-cool vibe. I chose a very pale warm gray for the walls and crisp white trim to make an airy background for the warm wood tones. The red undertones of the wood contrast with the green-gray glass tiles and khaki linen curtains. And a feast of grays—from stainless steel to polished quartz to felted upholstery fabric—creates an understated, professional look.

- To light up Cal's idea-generating dining/work space, I designed a fun and funky, custom-made, electrician-supervised, industrial light fixture—16 clear light bulbs suspended from a ceiling-mounted wood box and tied together like a bouquet of bright ideas!

RIGHT: Shaker-style cabinetry and distressed plank flooring balance the industrial feel of stainless-steel appliances and concrete-lookalike counters. A single, deep sink is super-practical in this limited space.

BACK IN THE BIG EASY

CHALLENGE

Although Cara and Anthony's kitchen was too cramped and cut off from the rest of the house, its real problem was what it *wasn't*—the family's dream kitchen, which they had just finished renovating in New Orleans when Hurricane Katrina hit. Although their house suffered only minor damage, the city's devastation pushed them to the difficult decision to leave their adopted home and take their two daughters back north, closer to their families. The couple loves to cook, eat, and entertain Southern style and what they wanted was a kitchen like the one they'd labored over and lost.

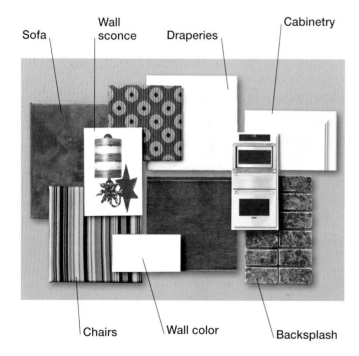

Sofa | Wall sconce | Draperies | Cabinetry

Chairs | Wall color | Backsplash

BEFORE: Cara and Anthony like to cook together, but they kept bumping into each other in this narrow, inconvenient kitchen. It was cut off from the rest of the house, but more important was the fact that it didn't feel like the New Orleans kitchen they'd lost—warm, cozy, and ready for entertaining.

AFTER: Furniture-style cabinetry with an unfitted look, wide-plank maple floors, and soapstone counters achieve a big-scale, Big-Easy makeover. Cabinetry doors conceal the refrigerator and freezer beside the stacked microwave, warming drawer, and oven. Separating the cooktop from the oven lets Cara and Anthony divide their tasks more easily when they're cooking up a Cajun-style feast.

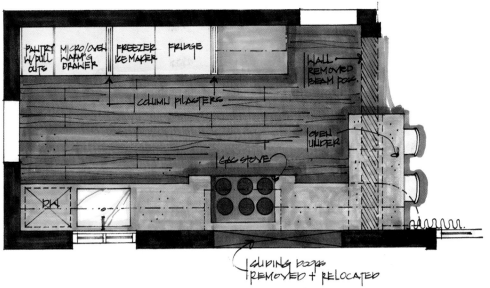

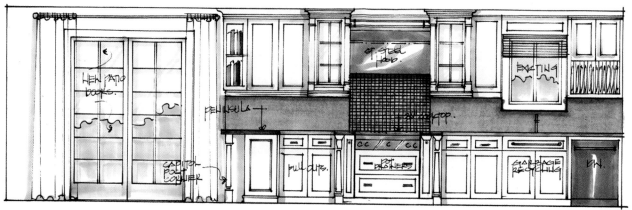

NORTH ELEVATION
1/2" = 1'-0"

SOLUTION

- Before I could give this kitchen some French Quarter finessing, the old cabinetry and flooring had to come out, along with the wall between the kitchen and the family room. In place of that wall, I designed a peninsula that would keep the two rooms open to each other and add a place for eating.

- To gain more wall space for new cabinetry, I bricked up the existing kitchen access to the backyard and relocated the sliding doors to the family room. Since the new, open kitchen-family room was now a little too open, I closed another doorway with a knee wall to create a nook for a corner sectional in the family room. I left the wall above open, as a pass-through that visually connects the spaces (see page 108).

- I found the perfect new cabinetry for instant Southern style—doors with molded, recessed panels and framing pilasters, turned furniture-style legs as accents, and a subtle antique finish. To tie the family room and the kitchen together, the cabinetry continues into the living room, where hutches flank the fireplace and a new mantel and surround give the fireplace the importance it deserves.

- For countertops with an old-world look, I chose soapstone. It's dense and durable, but what I love is how it oxidizes over time to develop a beautiful, gray-green patina. Since that process can take years, however, I recommend rubbing the surfaces with mineral oil monthly. This makes the stone oxidize 10 times faster!

- The same honed, matte-finish soapstone continues up the wall for the backsplash in most areas. To accent the area above the cooktop, I used soapstone mosaic tiles sealed with dark gray grout.

- New wide-plank maple flooring is perfect for evoking an old home in the French Quarter. The rich brown stain relates to the dark tone of the countertops, balancing the light color of the cabinetry and walls.

- New appliances add convenience and better function. The sink in front of the new window is super-deep, extra-wide, and has an integrated drainboard and ultra-modern pull-down faucet. Since I was going for an old-world look here, I hid the refrigerator and freezer behind cabinetry doors to avoid breaking up the woodwork with too much stainless steel (see page 105).

LIVING ROOM ELEVATION
1/2" = 1'-0"

OPPOSITE: A new peninsula with seating for two divides the kitchen from the family room without blocking views. The custom chandelier over the peninsula celebrates New Orleans with pendant sculptures made from materials salvaged after Hurricane Katrina. Under the gas cooktop, drawers provide storage for pots and pans.

ABOVE: Knocking down one wall opened the kitchen to the family room for better flow, while partially closing a door created a place to put new sectional seating. The pass-through above preserves the visual connection to the foyer.

OPPOSITE: The deep sink with an integrated drainboard recalls an old-fashioned farmhouse sink but in a modern material. Open storage, with a plate rack right above the dishwasher, is convenient as well as aesthetic—it puts dishes and cookware on display and helps the kitchen feel larger because your eye can travel past the cabinet frame. Soapstone counters and backsplash add an old-world feel.

STYLE ELEMENTS

- I chose a quiet, neutral palette for walls and cabinetry to play up the colors on the fabrics in the family room. A glazed antique wash on the cabinetry softens and warms up the white finish.

- To pay homage to the adopted city Cara and Anthony loved, I commissioned a New Orleans artist to create a custom light fixture for the new peninsula. Its classic lines and antique silver-leaf base capture the elegance of old New Orleans, while the little sculptures that hang from the arms evoke the flamboyance and fun of the French Quarter. Made from fragments found after Katrina, the sculptures also evoke the resilience and spirit of the city.

- For the new doors in the family room, I chose sliders that have integrated blinds (no dusting needed!) and a rolling screen door that lets fresh air in and keeps bugs out. Lovely for cool summer evenings!

- In the family room, a palette of warm, earthy tones plays out in solid velvet for the settee and stripes and modern geometrics for accents. Neutral linen curtains at the sliding doors blend in with the walls to put the focus on the spectacular lighting fixture.

FASHION-FORWARD FARMHOUSE KITCHEN

CHALLENGE

Crumbling cabinets, broken appliances, and a powder room in the kitchen—this stuck-in-the-1980s kitchen wasn't just a style disaster, it was a functional mess! Not at all what you'd expect from David, a professional style guru whose job is all about fashion and beauty. He had renovated much of the century-old farmhouse with his inimitable great taste, but the kitchen needed a complete makeover to become the functional and fashion-forward entertaining center he wanted. Plus it needed to serve as a home office and provide a sleeping spot for his favorite runway girls, pups Maggie and Mollie.

Quartz countertops   Backsplash   Wallpaper

Dog-bed fabric   Flooring

BEFORE: This 1980s kitchen was hopelessly out of date and a functional failure—the cooktop didn't work, the dishwasher threatened to fall apart, and cabinet doors were broken.

AFTER: A stylish blend of traditional and contemporary style, the new kitchen is roomy but functional, with clearly defined zones and plenty of space for cooking and entertaining.

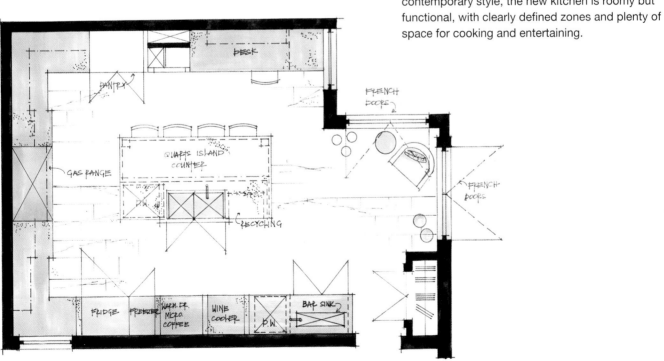

SOLUTION

- In order to accommodate all of David's diverse needs, I decided to completely reconfigure the space. Everything was cleared out—cabinets, appliances, powder room—even the old, leaking skylight in the ceiling was closed in. At one end of the room I added another set of French doors for better indoor-outdoor flow during parties.

- For the room's new centerpiece, I designed a high-style island, perfect for entertaining all of David's fashionista friends. This huge piece includes double sinks with an industrial-style faucet, a dishwasher, and a handy recycling center. The quartz countertop extends out on one side for relaxed bar-chair seating.

- All of the cooking and food-storage functions are gathered on the back wall of the new space. A pantry and lots of counter and cabinet space flank a six-burner gas range with double ovens and a griddle—ideal for the gourmet cooking David loves to do.

- On the adjacent perimeter wall, I designed a bar area, complete with a dual-temperature wine cooler, a built-in coffee maker, and a beautiful fridge and freezer column. The trough sink frees up counter space in addition to doubling as a handy ice bucket during parties.

- For David's home office, a built-in desk was installed between the window and the pantry. The shelf with task lighting and a storage unit with a chalkboard surface make this compact spot functional and efficient. Two stylish doggie beds fit snugly under the desk.

- For the floors I chose large-format travertine tiles in a light-reflecting cream color. They've been laid over a luxurious radiant heating system to keep feet and paws warm in winter.

RIGHT: The back wall of the kitchen is all about cooking. I chose traditional, oiled-bronze cabinetry hardware to pick up the color of the marble-tile backsplash and dark-wood island.

A complete bar and beverage center includes a wine refrigerator and a built-in coffee maker. Below the coffee maker I included a microwave and warming drawer. The upper cabinets were painted black inside and fitted with spotlights and glass doors for a dramatic display of David's stemware and ceramics collection.

STYLE ELEMENTS

- I felt the kitchen should marry traditional style with contemporary, to suit the character of the house and still reflect David's fashion-forward sensibility. For the perimeter walls, I chose creamy recessed-panel cabinets with an antique strié finish that references the period of the house.

- To give the island the look of fine furniture, I designed it with traditional raised-panel doors, furniture-style feet, and turned posts for the dining-side corners. A pair of crystal chandeliers above it definitely turn up the glam factor!

- Mushroom-color quartz countertops and brown marble backsplash tiles help balance all of the creamy cabinetry and floor tiles.

- The desk area is the first thing you see when you come into the kitchen, so it needed to have a real "wow" factor. Because there were so many cabinets on the other walls, I decided to keep the wall space open and dress it in silver foil wallpaper with a dramatic large-scale medallion pattern—a fashion-conscious nod to the home's traditional vintage.

LEFT: Every pantry needs pull-out shelves—no more lost cans of pâté! Blackboard paint on the adjacent cabinet turns the door into a message board.

OPPOSITE: The desk wall is the first thing you see when you enter the kitchen, so it had to be a showstopper. This large-scale wallpaper printed on silver foil makes the right modern yet nostalgic impact. Halogen lights mounted under the wall shelf illuminate the desk surface, and recessed ceiling lights provide general lighting.

LOFTY AMBITIONS

CHALLENGE

The loft conversion in this 100-year-old downtown warehouse had terrific character and space—except in the kitchen. A surprisingly tiny U-shaped cooking area had little storage, poor-quality laminate countertops, backsplash tiles intended for a bathroom—and awful mauve-pink walls. Single-in-the-city Nalini wasn't a big fan of the open-shelf cabinetry either, but she loved the traditional flooring, the exposed posts and ceiling pipes, and the brand-new appliances. She enjoys being able to interact with her guests while she's cooking, and she loves a mix of old and new—she wants it all! Can she have it? Yes!

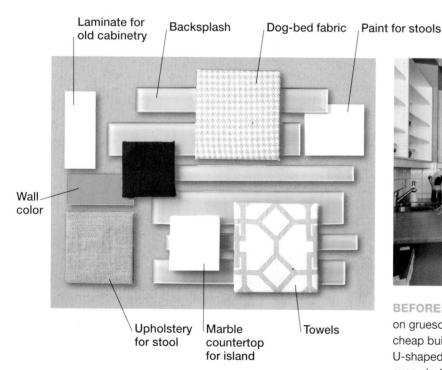

Laminate for old cabinetry · Backsplash · Dog-bed fabric · Paint for stools · Wall color · Upholstery for stool · Marble countertop for island · Towels

BEFORE: The kitchen in this loft was short on style and long on gruesome pink walls! The appliances were brand-new, but cheap builder finishes, inadequate storage, and a cramped U-shaped layout discouraged first-time homeowner Nalini from even starting to unpack.

AFTER: Stretching the U into an L extended both the floor space and the function. A fabulous antique cabinet repurposed as an island adds eating space, storage, and work space. The old cabinets were retrofitted and refaced to match new Shaker-style cabinets along the reconfigured sink wall.

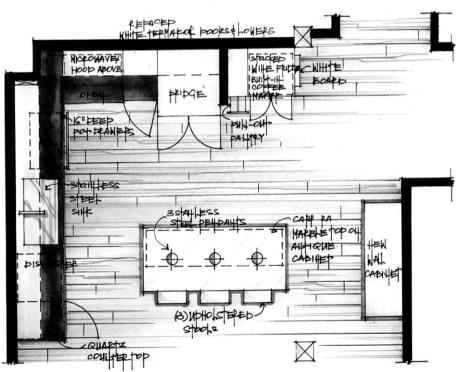

REFACED WHITE THERMAFOIL DOORS & LOWERS

MICROWAVE HOOD ABOVE

STOCKED WHITE FRIDGE

WHITE BOARD

OVEN

FRIDGE

BUILT-IN COFFEE MAKER

16" DEEP POT DRAWERS

PULL-OUT PANTRY

3 STAINLESS STEEL SINK

3 STAINLESS STEEL PENDANTS

CARRARA MARBLE TOP ON ANTIQUE CABINET

NEW WALL CABINET

DISHWASHER

(3) UPHOLSTERED STOOLS

QUARTZ COUNTER TOP

SOLUTION

- To give Nalini more elbow room, I changed the U-shaped layout into an open L-shape. Borrowing a little space from the living room, I installed additional cabinets in line with the existing ones to provide more storage and a more efficient location for the dishwasher and a new stainless-steel sink.

- Although the old, existing cabinets were new, they just weren't Nalini's style so I had all of the doors removed and the exposed frames of the cabinets refaced with new laminate. Both existing and newly added cabinets were then fronted with Shaker-style doors. Shaker style blends a traditional feeling with contemporary straight lines, so it's a perfect mix of the old and new that appeals to Nalini.

- Polished quartz countertops look like brushed stainless steel, a nod to the stainless appliances and the industrial feel of the loft.

- A new glass-tile backsplash that continues above the cabinets brings in a sleek modern finish and a hint of texture. The translucent quality of glass tiles also gives the walls more depth, a plus in this space.

- For the centerpiece of the new kitchen, I wanted an antique piece of furniture that could be repurposed as an island. I found just the thing, an 8-foot-long mahogany-stained cabinet with tons of drawers on one side. I topped it with a thick slab of classic Carrara marble that extends deep enough on one side for bar-stool seating. To support the extension, I had a pair of legs and apron custom-made to match the cabinet.

- The oven, microwave, and fridge stayed put, but to turn up the modern vibe, I added a beverage center with a built-in coffee maker and state-of-the-art wine fridge.

RIGHT: This end-wall space was begging for something to do, so I installed cabinetry with pull-out storage and tucked in a wine fridge and coffee maker. Coffee, anyone?

ABOVE: Polished quartz countertops pick up the warm gray color on the condo walls. For a hip, high-tech look, I paired a gorgeous stainless-steel, bevel-edge sink with a super-cool articulated faucet. Its five pivoting joints allow Nalini to direct water exactly where she wants it. Green glass tiles of varying widths add texture and a pop of subtle color. Note how the horizontal orientation helps visually stretch the space!

ABOVE: Since you can never have too much storage, I placed a free-standing hutch on the wall opposite the kitchen. It has the same Shaker-style doors as the kitchen cabinets, but instead of opening out, the doors slide from side to side, a practical space-saving option.

STYLE ELEMENTS

- Getting rid of that awful pink wall color was a top priority! I covered all of the pink with the same deep, warm gray that was in the entrance hall and chose crisp white cabinetry for a bright, fresh contrast. I painted Nalini's old bar stools white, too, and topped them with thick cushions upholstered in a light neutral fabric so her guests have a comfy place to perch.

- For a little punch of color, I chose light green glass tiles with snowy white, unsanded grout. The green is a soft, pretty hue that looks cool and refreshing with the white cabinets and gray walls.

- Playing contemporary off of traditional, I chose three industrial-style stainless-steel pendant lamps to hang above the island. They're fitted with frosted diffusers to eliminate glare for anyone sitting or working at the island.

- Inside the display cabinets, I added mirror backing to reflect light. The only windows in the loft are at the opposite end of the room, so light-enhancing tricks like this, along with under-cabinet lighting and track lights, help keep the space from feeling cavelike.

RIGHT: Three rows of drawers provide loads of great storage for Nalini. Drawer divider kits partition off space inside the shallow drawers to make organizing flatware and utensils easier.

CITY STYLE IN SUBURBIA

CHALLENGE

When my most trusted design supervisor, Steven, and his partner, Allen, moved from their city condo to a bungalow in the 'burbs, they worried that their city friends might not come visit. And if they *did* come visit, what would they think when they saw the sad, outdated state of this fixer-upper? It needed more work than the pair had originally thought, and with Steven's hectic work schedule, Allen feared it would take him months working by himself to get things in shape. To show Steven how much I value everything he does, I offered to lend a hand and bring some hip city style to their new suburban home.

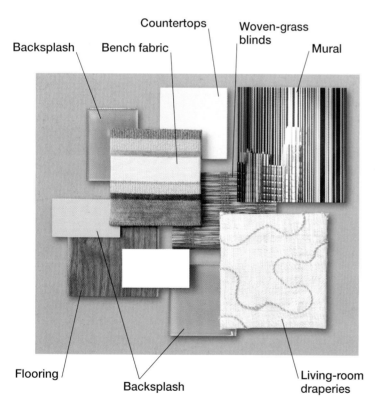

Backsplash · Bench fabric · Countertops · Woven-grass blinds · Mural

Flooring · Backsplash · Living-room draperies

BEFORE: Outdated cabinets and backsplash tiles, cotton-candy pink walls, and country-cute wallpaper borders definitely did *not* look like the kind of kitchen Steven and Allen would cook or entertain in. At least, not without being blindfolded!

FRIDGE COOKTOP

AREA CARPET

WINE FRIDGE WALL OVEN DISH WASHER SINK

AFTER: Ahh, now this is more like it! Sleek, dark-wood cabinetry with creamy quartz counters and gleaming stainless-steel appliances instantly says hip urban style. A super-cool gooseneck faucet with stick-shift control converts to a sprayer when you pull down the nozzle. The dishwasher is to the right of the sink, hidden behind a cabinet panel.

SOLUTION

- The first floor was chopped up into little rooms, so to create a better flow for entertaining, I started by taking out walls and making one big space. With new drywall, new hardwood floors, and new ceilings, the entire first floor was ready for zoning. Furniture arrangement and focal points define the new living and dining areas. Cabinetry and dropped pendant lights define the kitchen.

- Contemporary slab-front cabinets with sleek drawer pulls provide a ton of much-needed storage space.

- Steven and Allen love the high-tech, modern look, so naturally the appliances are stainless steel—a side-by-side fridge and freezer on one side and a wall oven, microwave, and warming drawer stacked opposite. A built-in wine fridge anchors a small seating area at the end of the room.

- The sleek induction cooktop truly is high-tech—it uses electricity to generate an electromagnetic field that causes the pot or pan to heat up. Water boils in 60 seconds, and when you remove the pan, the cooktop is cool to the touch. (You can only use iron or steel pots on this type of cooktop—copper, aluminum, and glass aren't magnetic and won't react.)

- A glass-tile backsplash adds some luminous depth to the walls, and quartz counters provide hardworking surfaces for food prep.

- Good design is green design, so I included a recycling center with pull-out bins to hold cans, paper, and bottles.

ABOVE: A stylized mural of the city adds some "wow" factor to the end wall. With a wine fridge on the left and more storage and counter space on the right, this area serves as a staging ground for party preparations.

LEFT: The glass-tile backsplash picks up colors used in the living room. The smooth induction cooktop is truly high-tech, using electromagnetic energy for super-fast cooking.

STYLE ELEMENTS

- The high contrast between dark wood cabinets and warm white counters provides the downtown vibe this kitchen needed. I used a minimum of hardware to avoid breaking up the clean planes of the cabinet doors. I even hid the dishwasher behind a cabinet door to preserve a unified, minimalist look.

- Two backsplashes of varying-width glass tiles bring the calm, cool color scheme from the living area into the kitchen. Alternating bands of blue, green, and taupe create a crisp, linear effect (orderly and organized, just like Steven!).

- To turn the end wall into a dramatic focal point, I had a graphics company enlarge a stylized image of a city skyline at night and applied it as a mural.

- A bar-height glass table and a pair of bar stools don't take up much space visually or physically but provide a spot for morning coffee or spillover seating for parties.

Glass pendants and slightly taller end cabinets help set the kitchen apart from the dining area. Usually I like to repeat the countertop color on the floor, but here I unified the whole main floor with the same hardwood flooring, so I used a light-color area rug to achieve the same effect.

DRESSED FOR SUCCESS

CHALLENGE

This small, outdated kitchen needed a rapid-fire makeover in time for two big deliveries: Homeowners Tova and Daniel were expecting their first child; and Daniel, a video game developer, would soon be launching his company's latest game. They're a hip and stylish young couple, and the dated, dysfunctional kitchen and adjoining living room didn't reflect their style or suit their needs for entertaining. Plus, they desperately needed more storage—half the kitchen supplies were downstairs in a makeshift pantry—and a more functional, efficient layout for food prep and cleanup.

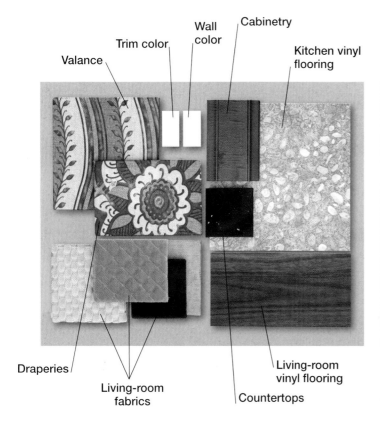

Valance • Trim color • Wall color • Cabinetry • Kitchen vinyl flooring

Draperies • Living-room fabrics • Countertops • Living-room vinyl flooring

BEFORE: This tiny eat-in kitchen was a typical 1980s builder-box space, with ceramic tile floors, laminate cabinetry, and faux butcher-block countertops. It reflected nothing of the personality of its young, modern owners.

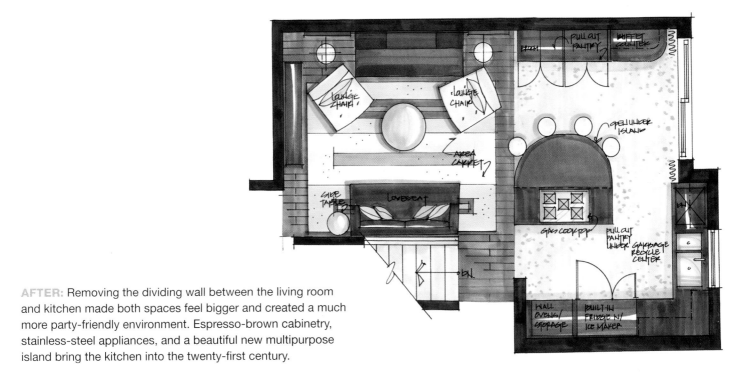

AFTER: Removing the dividing wall between the living room and kitchen made both spaces feel bigger and created a much more party-friendly environment. Espresso-brown cabinetry, stainless-steel appliances, and a beautiful new multipurpose island bring the kitchen into the twenty-first century.

SOLUTION

- There wasn't much that was salvageable in this kitchen, so to bring it into the twenty-first century I started from scratch, ripping out all of the cabinets, flooring, fixtures, and appliances. And to steal more space for the kitchen, the partial wall that divided the kitchen and living room was knocked out to create one big, open area. Now Tova and Daniel have a clear sightline all the way from the living room through the kitchen to views of the beautiful backyard.

- Tova and Daniel needed more storage, so I incorporated the old eating area into the new kitchen floor plan. A new bank of floor-to-ceiling cabinets and a built-in buffet fill the empty wall in the old eating area, adding oodles of storage for pots, pans, and food as well as a counter for setting out drinks and appetizers.

- New cabinetry along the back and side walls wraps the kitchen in rich, dark wood. A new stainless-steel sink under the window keeps the view the old sink had, but now Tova has two stainless-steel dishwashers— one beside the sink and one in the island for no-hassle cleanup after big parties. On the adjoining wall, a spacious, 42-inch, counter-depth stainless-steel refrigerator and two stacked wall ovens (one a microwave and the other a convection oven) give Chef Tova maximum functionality in a minimum of space.

- I relocated most of the cooking functions to a much larger island. The five-burner cooktop is just a few steps from the sink and refrigerator with ample room behind should two people be cooking at once. The island also provides additional storage as well as a roomy counter for eating that takes the place of the previous cramped table and chairs.

- New vinyl tile flooring in a river-stone pattern helps hide small spills and dust and adds soft, warm neutral color underfoot.

STYLE ELEMENTS

- Tova and Daniel wanted a new-millennium look with lots of dark wood and stainless steel, so I chose espresso-brown cabinetry with recessed-panel doors. The cabinets reflect the look of fine traditional furniture and are sophisticated without being fussy.

- Hardworking black quartz countertops continue up the wall to form the backsplash. The dark color and seamless counter-backsplash detail set off the stainless-steel appliances and balance the traditional elements with a more contemporary feel. Waterfall-style bar chairs, a sleek stainless-steel and glass range hood, and an ultra-modern sink faucet tilt the overall look toward fresh, modern style.

- To keep this open-concept kitchen looking open, I chose glass for the range hood above the cooktop rather than stainless steel, which would have looked too big and clunky. Glass range hoods are visually lighter and streamlined and less obtrusive when situated above an island.

ABOVE: Mounting the box-pleated window valance on the ceiling continues the line of the cabinetry and gives the illusion of added height. A black woven shade pulls down for privacy and light control and relates the window to the color of the counters and backsplash.

- To bring in some color and softness, I framed the sliding glass doors with simple fabric panels. The bold pattern brings visual relief and interest to all the solid surfaces, but the muted colors blend the panels with the cabinetry. Over the sink window, a smaller-scale coordinate suits the proportions of the valance.

- Although this new kitchen was now completely open to the living room and much more suitable for entertaining, I had to ensure that the two spaces flowed together visually. A quick and simple update involving a slipper chair, accent fabrics, and accessories in a color scheme of brown, green, blue, and beige ties the two rooms together while defining each as a separate zone—one for cooking, eating, and conversation, and the other for watching TV, playing Daniel's video games, and visiting with friends.

ABOVE: Elegant floor-to-bulkhead cabinetry stores pots, pans, and pantry items along one wall. A buffet tucked into the corner near the patio door offers counter space for serving—especially handy for indoor-outdoor parties! (Note the second dishwasher in the end of the island—perfect to help with a quick cleanup after a big party!)

THE COOKIE QUEEN'S KITCHEN

CHALLENGE

After twenty years of constant use, this 1960s kitchen was hungry for transformation. Ziba is an insatiable cook and loves to bake—in fact, she bakes morning, noon, and night and is even known to get up at 3 a.m. to mix up a batch of cookies! Her poor, tired kitchen simply couldn't keep up. It had plenty of space but was woefully short on function and style. There was too little counter space, the faux wood cabinets couldn't hold all of her cookware, and there were too many doors chopping up the walls. She loves to entertain, but the idea of inviting guests over into this outdated room made Ziba cringe!

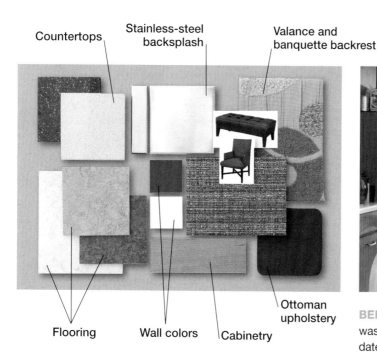

Countertops

Stainless-steel backsplash

Valance and banquette backrest

Flooring

Wall colors

Cabinetry

Ottoman upholstery

BEFORE: After twenty years of hard use, this 1960s kitchen was stuck in a time warp, with worn-out appliances and a tired, dated look. Five doors to adjoining rooms chopped up the walls and robbed Ziba of potential storage and counter space.

AFTER: Closing up two doors created a long wall for a built-in refrigerator, new cabinets, and a wraparound peninsula that provides a sea of counter space. Warm cherrywood cabinets with a mix of frosted-glass and slab-front doors create the clean, contemporary look Ziba wanted.

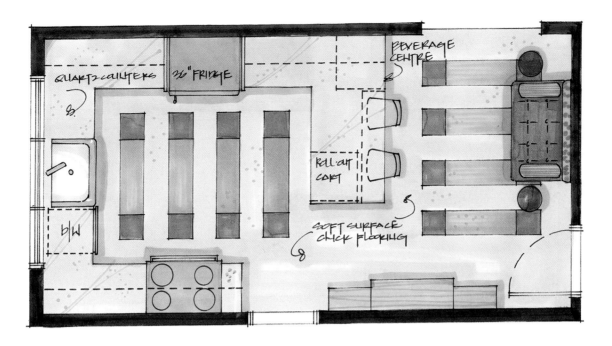

QUARTZ COUNTERS

36" FRIDGE

BEVERAGE CENTRE

ROLL-OUT CART

SOFT SURFACE CHICK FLOORING

D/W

135

SOLUTION

- The old cabinets, counters, appliances, and parquet flooring all had to go! I closed up two doors and carved out a large, arched opening at the back of the room. This connects the kitchen to the dining room, creating one flowing space that's much better for entertaining.

- Where the two doors had been, I placed a new wraparound peninsula with a deep counter and seating. The seating side helps define a small lounge area at the back of the kitchen, just off the dining room—perfect for parties and gatherings.

- Beautiful cherry cabinets in a much more functional layout provide tons of storage for all of Ziba's cookware and baking supplies. To keep all of the wood from feeling too heavy, I designed a mixture of both slab fronts and frosted glass doors. Illuminated by in-cabinet lighting, the glass doors give the kitchen the clean, modern look Ziba wanted.

- Stretches of quartz countertops provide plenty of room for mixing up cakes and cookies. To give Ziba even more work space, I designed a baking island on wheels that tucks under the peninsula when not in use. The marble top is just the right height for rolling out pastry dough, and frosted-glass doors turn the shelving underneath into closed storage space. (A good place to hide a pan of brownies!)

- All the open floor space offered a perfect blank canvas for a fabulous flooring product. A hipper distant relative of linoleum, this floor comes in a roll format or as large planks that simply snap together in place. The surface is softer underfoot than tile or stone and is a great choice if you're standing in the kitchen for long periods of time. It's also unique in that the color (and there are a zillion of them!) goes all the way through and the material is self healing, so scratches or scrapes simply disappear.

- To balance out the warmth of the cherry cabinets, I chose cool stainless steel for the backsplash, the apron-front sink, and state-of-the-art appliances. With all the heavy-duty baking Ziba does, nothing less than an industrial-size range would do, and the built-in barbeque expands her options for party menus.

RIGHT: A deep, oversize stainless-steel apron-front sink is great for filling big pots of water as well as for washing stacks of cookie sheets and mixing bowls. The undermount installation makes it easy to sweep crumbs and spills off the counter and into the sink.

ABOVE: To accommodate Ziba's nearly round-the-clock baking, I installed an industrial-size oven with a gas range and built-in barbeque. Cabinetry features tons of storage for cookware, spices, and baking ingredients—the lower corner cupboard pulls out to reveal full-access shelves, and the cabinet to the left of the range hides pull-out spice shelves. Open shelving is stainless-steel laminate, more affordable and easier to install than stainless-steel shelving.

STYLE ELEMENTS

- I wanted a very warm theme for Ziba's new kitchen, so I picked up the undertones of yellow and orange in the cherry wood and used those to guide the selection of colors for walls, counters, and flooring.

- A wheat-tone paint on the side walls speaks to the warm undertones of the wood and also relates to the wall color in the adjoining dining room. To heat up the scheme even more, I chose a spicy tomato red for the end walls.

- Buttery quartz counters pull out the yellow note in the wood. Quartz comes in more colors than granite or marble, and I wanted a specific color to work with the wood undertones in Ziba's kitchen.

- To keep the horizontal surfaces in the same tones, I chose a lighter version of buttery yellow for the flooring. To give the floor some visual interest, I had bands of contrasting color inset down the length of the room. The bands bring the cabinetry color down to the floor with lighter and darker shades of the wood, and they give the illusion of making the kitchen seem wider.

- The fabric used for the valance has a retro green, yellow, and orange scheme and helps soften the window. Installing the valance at the ceiling continues the line of the cabinetry and makes the window look taller (see page 135).

- For the new lounge area at the back of the kitchen, I designed a comfy ottoman upholstered in spicy red. The retro valance fabric repeats on the upholstered backrest, helping tie the space together.

- I added lots of lighting to illuminate all the counters, cabinets, and work zones. Recessed lighting follows the perimeter of the room, and undercabinet lights shine down on the countertops and make the stainless-steel backsplashes gleam. Lights inside the glass-front cabinets add to the glow. Over the peninsula, I hung very chic pendants with enclosed frosted glass shades. When Ziba and her family are sitting at the counter eating cupcakes—no glare!

ABOVE: A comfy ottoman with an upholstered backrest turns the back wall into a lounge for Ziba's guests. Warm tomato red (painted over a tinted primer base) turns this wall into a focal point.

OPPOSITE: Built to look like a freestanding hutch, a cabinetry unit in the lounge area provides more storage as well as a serving area for parties.

A new, wide, arched opening at one end of the room creates a better flow between the dining room and the kitchen. The new peninsula divides Ziba's work space from the lounge area. With a below-the-counter microwave and pull-out baker's island, the peninsula is more than just a pretty face—it's a super-functional prep zone and eating counter. Floor planks made of a linoleum-like material click together for a seamless look.

A FRESH KITCHEN FACELIFT

CHALLENGE

This tiny kitchen and adjoining dining area had the potential to be a great space for entertaining, and the appliances and cabinets were in good shape. But the cabinet color, the salmon countertops, and white tile walls were stuck in the eighties, decades away from the casual, contemporary tastes of newlyweds and new homeowners Martin and Emily. They didn't have a big budget to work with, so the challenge would be to update, adapt, and put the decorating dollars where they would have the most impact.

Draperies   Backsplash

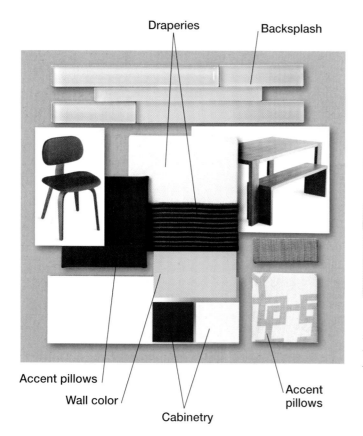

Accent pillows

Wall color

Cabinetry

Accent pillows

BEFORE: The honeymoon was over for this tiny kitchen. With salmon pink countertops, pink-toned cabinets and dated tile walls, it was stuck in the eighties and totally out of step with the tastes of new homeowners and newlyweds Martin and Emily.

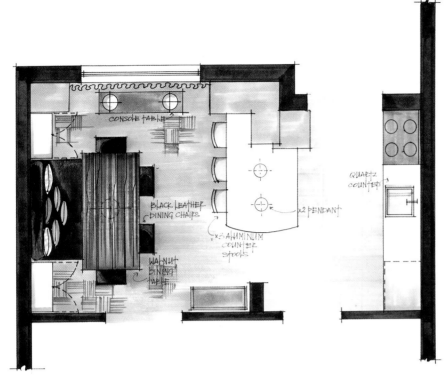

CONSOLE TABLE

BLACK LEATHER DINING CHAIRS

x3 ALUMINUM COUNTER STOOLS

WALNUT DINING TABLE

x2 PENDANT

QUARTZ COUNTER

AFTER: Painting the cabinets and walls, replacing the countertops, and installing a stunning glass-tile backsplash transformed the kitchen into a model of casual contemporary style. A new, modern sink and high-tech jointed faucet also helped lift the space out its dated doldrums.

SOLUTION

- Paint is your best friend when you want to update an old kitchen inexpensively. Martin and Emily liked the soft blue-gray they'd used in the dining room, so I borrowed that color for the kitchen walls. I even painted over the tile beside the oven to help stretch the budget.

- Taking my cue from the dishwasher and oven, I painted the lower cabinets black to match, creating a unified, custom-finished look. A coat of white on the upper cabinets and peninsula lightened and brightened the space, and painting the bulkhead white as well stretched the cabinets visually to the ceiling. Adding white crown molding helps give the stock cabinets the look of high-end custom cabinets . . . a great budget-stretching trick!

- New jewel-like hardware in silver and black dresses up the traditional cabinets with a modern accent.

- The sink elevation is what you see from the dining room, so I decided to install a new backsplash that would really give the space some character. You know the wedding saying, "Something old, something new, something borrowed, something blue"? Well, for these newlyweds, the backsplash is both the new and the blue! Removing the two small, center cabinets to give the wall a more open feeling, I had beautiful blue glass tiles installed in a random pattern. The tile pulls in the wall color and adds shimmer and depth to the space. Open shelving between the remaining cabinets allows for display without covering up the tile.

- New quartz countertops in a subtle taupe color have flecks of silver and recycled bottle glass to bring in the colors of the stainless steel refrigerator and the walls. The new peninsula countertop is slightly more generous than the old one was—it extends into the dining room and gives Martin and Emily a breakfast area as well as more work space.

- I put in a new under-mount sink for a more modern look and installed a totally cool jointed faucet for a real conversation piece! (It's also very functional.)

- New halogen track lighting and some puck lights over the sink eliminate shadows and put light where it's needed for cooking and cleanup. Modern pendants over the peninsula illuminate the work/eat space.

- To help tie the dining room and kitchen together, I brought the look of the kitchen cabinets into the dining room with two new storage pieces. They only appear built-in—they're actually assembled from modular cabinets, with two glass-front cabinets stacked on top of a closed cupboard for each unit.

- For the feature wall in the dining room, I painted the area between the new cupboards with blackboard paint and hung a huge, funky mirror over it. The blackboard wall is the most inexpensive art possible—when friends and family come over, they can get out the chalk and draw!

- The space between the cupboards was perfect for a banquette that would double as dining table seating, but a new banquette wasn't in the budget.

ABOVE: Eames-style chairs and a contemporary walnut table are modern classics that won't go out of style. For extra seating at the dining table, I made a banquette from a leather and chrome ottoman raised on a platform.

So I took a leather and chrome ottoman, raised it on a wooden platform, and added colorful pillows to make it comfy for guests.

- Vertical fabric blinds hide windows that have seen better days, but for a dressier look, I framed the windows with customized curtain panels. They're made from two sets of readymade cotton panels, one black and one white. The black panels were cut up and used to trim the bottom and leading edge of the white panels. Install oversize grommets along the top edge, thread over a pole, and voilà! Fabulous custom draperies!

- To bring a little elegance to the space, I found a beautiful chandelier that's a clean, contemporary interpretation of a traditional shape. Just the right touch for this happily-ever-after heart of the home.

BELOW: To unify the kitchen and dining room as a single space, new cabinetry assembled from modular pieces brings kitchen storage functions into the dining room. Blackboard paint turns the wall into do-it-yourself art. A blend of traditional touches and modern furniture creates a style that can evolve and grow over time.

BATHS

3 MASTER SUITE SPACES

LOFTY RETREAT

CHALLENGE

Renovating a 100-year-old row house in the city seemed like a great idea to Barb and Evan, who were tired of their two-hour commute from the suburbs. They bought the house and began gutting it with gusto. Now, a year later, they had done a lot of tearing down but not much building up. With dwindling funds, drained energy, and vanishing patience, they were desperate for some help. I came in to turn the third floor into a loftlike master bedroom and en suite bath to help this exhausted couple kick-start completion of the whole-house reno.

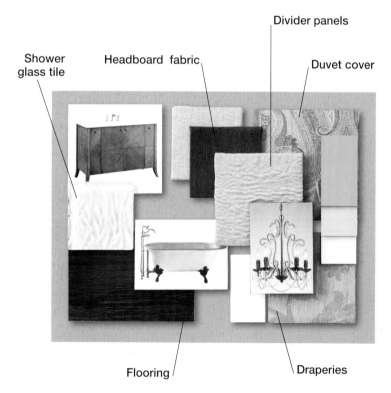

Shower glass tile · Headboard fabric · Divider panels · Duvet cover · Flooring · Draperies

BEFORE: Barb and Evan got the third floor stripped back to the studs and new ductwork installed, but with limited time and funds, they were a long way from making this a space for sweet dreams.

AFTER: I divided the space into a master bedroom and bath with a central cube that contains the shower, a toilet compartment, and closets. Textured gold fabric panels mounted on the ceiling alongside the shower can be drawn across to screen the bath for privacy when needed. They stack flat against the wall otherwise (as you see here). Wood-look vinyl flooring offers the warm, rich appearance of wood with the benefits of a waterproof surface.

ABOVE: A 700-pound cast-iron claw-foot tub pays homage to the home's vintage character. (And the handheld shower head is great for karaoke!) Textures like the woven wood blinds, silk draperies, and wood vanity bring warmth and a sense of comfort to the space. Sconces with shades add a dressy, formal accent over the vanity, and recessed ceiling fixtures provide even ambient lighting throughout the space.

SOLUTION

- Since Barb and Evan already had the third floor stripped down to the studs and insulation, I could start right in, putting in subflooring, drywall, and trim work. Then it was time to shape the space.

- I divided the bedroom from the bath area with a short wall of closets, which also serve as an acoustical buffer between the rooms. I lined one entire wall of the bedroom area with closets to give Barb and Evan loads of storage space.

- Behind the short wall of closets, I tucked in a separate compartment for the toilet.

- In the remaining area, at the head of the stairs, I placed a shower unit adjoining the toilet compartment and a cast-iron footed tub on the opposite wall. The floor had to be reinforced to support the weight of the tub—complete with feet, it weighed in at 700 pounds, and that's without the water! Getting it up three flights of stairs was no easy task, but it was worth it—together with the vanity, it forms the focal point of the third-floor area and pays homage to the vintage character of the house.

- To create a continuous flow from bathroom to bedroom, I used the same flooring throughout, a dark vinyl that mimics wood but is waterproof. Water and wood—never a good combination!

OPPOSITE: This fabulous sink was a near-perfect match for the fabric that inspired the entire decorating scheme in Barb and Evan's new master bedroom suite. A white quartz countertop sets it off beautifully. I chose a vintage-style faucet and porcelain handles to pick up on the style of the tub.

RIGHT: A beautiful green glass tile accents the back of the quartz-walled shower. A bench in the shower is a little touch of luxury and if it's custom-crafted, it costs big bucks. A fully integrated shower unit, on the other hand, offers the comfort of a molded seat at a much more affordable price.

STYLE ELEMENTS

- I needed a jumping-off point for choosing finishes, fabrics, and colors, and found it in a box marked "Barb's favorite fabrics." A beautiful sage-green-and-gold embroidered cloth pointed me toward a palette of grayed sage and soft blue for the walls, snowy white for trim and fixtures, and a range of sages, super-pale blues, and gold for the draperies, privacy screen, and bedding.

- I found a spectacular porcelain sink for the vanity that matched the fabric almost perfectly—incredible! Dropped into a prefab vanity with a white quartz countertop, the sink gives the piece a custom look without the expense of custom fabrication.

- The fabric also inspired the accent tile for the shower, a beautiful green 4×4-inch glass tile with a rippled, watery surface.

- For privacy in the bath area, I installed a screen of fabric panels in a ceiling-mounted track. The panels pull across for a subtle, soft wall of privacy when needed and otherwise stack flat against the outside wall of the shower.

- Woven wood blinds provide privacy and light control at the windows, but to bring in more softness I framed the window at the head of the stairs with beautiful silk draperies. It's the same fabric that's on the bed coverlet, helping tie the two spaces together.

- Barb and Evan's king-size bed takes up most of the space in the bedroom, so I centered it under the windows and designed an upholstered headboard to give it more presence. A hollow-core door covered with thick upholstery foam and brown linen provides support for stacks of pillows—perfect for reading in bed. A mini-chandelier over the bed, along with bedding and pillows in textiles inspired by Barb's favorite fabric, creates a luxurious and elegant look.

ABOVE: Tucked between the closets (on the right) and the shower (on the left), the toilet compartment offers privacy in an otherwise open-concept suite. A built-in niche provides handy storage.

OPPOSITE: A new upholstered headboard and elegant bedding create a sumptuous focal point for the master bedroom. To create a feeling of continuity in this open-concept space, the same wall color flows from bathroom into bedroom.

GLASS ACT

CHALLENGE

Empty-nesters Tony and Sasha love their home and have no intention of downsizing. In fact, they want to enjoy every inch of it, including the once-upon-a-time granny suite on the third floor. Although they didn't need the tiny kitchen or pokey little bath and the 1980s décor had long passed its best-by date, the space was bright and airy, flooded with natural light. It seemed perfect for a new, luxurious master bedroom and bath suite—with the emphasis on a truly dreamy bath. Both Sasha and Tony are avid cyclists, and Tony wanted a shower with a bench so he could shave his legs for biking—yup, it was Tony who requested this! Sasha's priority was a wonderful bathtub for long, relaxing soaks.

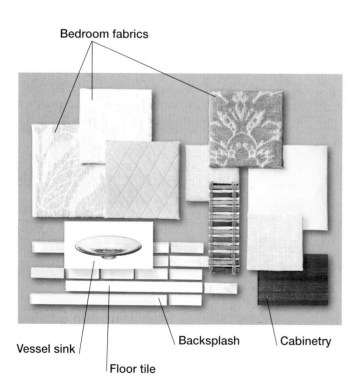

Bedroom fabrics

Vessel sink

Floor tile

Backsplash

Cabinetry

BEFORE: The bathroom in Tony and Sasha's third-floor "granny suite" had seen its best-by date come and go. The space no longer functioned the way they needed it to, and they were ready for a change.

AFTER: A sumptuous bathroom now divides the master bedroom at one end from a capacious dressing room and closet area at the other. A scheme of watery greens and blues set off by crisp white creates an open, airy, ahhh-spa feeling.

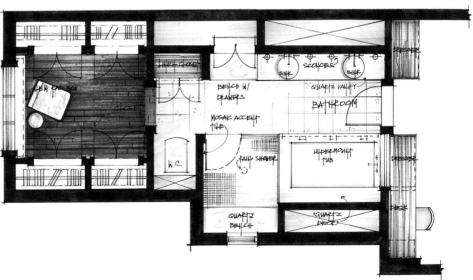

SOLUTION

- Before I could make any dreams come true, I had to gut the entire third floor, front to back, down to the studs. That left a big open space, most of it under high, steeply angled ceilings. Once the new insulation, drywall, and recessed lighting were in place, I divided the space into three zones: a large dressing room full of closets at one end, an elegant, light-filled bedroom at the other, and a sumptuous bathroom in between.

- I nestled Sasha's deep soaker tub under the roof angle with a skylight above to bring in more light. An extra-wide quartz deck provides space for a wine glass and candles—after all, this tub is about relaxation!

- On the opposite wall, a long vanity with his and hers sinks and storage for toiletries provides generous space for grooming.

- Beside the tub, an extra-roomy shower offers Tony his beloved bench as well as a rain shower head and wall-mounted hand shower. The frameless glass enclosure keeps the whole bathroom feeling open and light.

- Along the vanity wall, I added a linen closet and a bench with drawers below—storage galore!

- For the floors, I chose a gorgeous figured marble tile that resembles rippled water. Slabs of clean, unpatterned quartz for the vanity, shower walls, and tub deck set off the floor tile. To pull it all together, I found a backsplash tile that mixes off-cuts of the floor tile with white marble—a perfect marriage!

- When it comes to toilets, there are toilets—and then there are *toilets*. The proverbial throne in this new bathroom uses little water, lowers the seat and lid by itself, flushes automatically, and even glows with LED lighting! (Now if it would only clean itself . . .!)

OPPOSITE: A stained-glass window made by Sasha drove the decisions for finishes and colors. A beautiful tile mosaic, made from off-cuts of the floor tile and a pure white marble tile, accents the wall and bench. Waterproof lights set into the bench add to the atmosphere.

LEFT: A custom-cut window wall divides the bedroom from the bath, sharing light between the two spaces. The built-in dressing table matches the bathroom cabinetry, unifying the two rooms.

A deep soaker tub with a broad quartz deck invites hours of luxurious soaking. Waterproof lights set into the wall and tub surround add ambient light. A new skylight brings in natural light to supplement light borrowed from the bedroom through the end-wall window and door.

STYLE ELEMENTS

- Sasha is a talented stained-glass artist, and I wanted to use one of her pieces as a touchstone for the entire renovation. A window with a tulip design inspired the color scheme for the third-floor space and became a focal point in the shower, where I centered it on the wall over the bench.

- The window's watery greens and blues found their way into the room in the super-pale gray-green floor tile, the backsplash, the vessel sinks, and accent fabrics. Crisp white quartz for the vanity, tub deck, and shower walls sets off the figured marble flooring and creates a clean, contemporary feel.

- Above the sinks, I had large frameless mirrors installed to fit snugly between the countertop and the low ceiling line. For an ultra-sleek look, the spout faucets and taps are mounted through the mirrors.

- To ground this light, bright atmosphere, I chose a warm walnut stain for the vanity and built-in bench. Dark wood takes the hard edge off of a contemporary space and balances it with a touch of traditional style.

- Layers of light really define this space. Natural light pours in through skylights, the stained-glass feature window, and borrowed light from the bedroom. Chrome sconces blend modern and traditional—the straight lines and chrome material are contemporary, while the torch-inspired shape and fabric shades are traditional. At the tub, waterproof fixtures set into the surround and the wall above create moody light for Sasha to soak by—and pretty backlighting for her glass of wine!

ABOVE: Set into its own compartment, this proverbial throne is a low-flow model with automatic seat and lid closure, automatic flush, and LED lighting. Now that's luxurious!

ABOVE: This is the perfect sink for this bathroom—a textured-glass vessel that resembles the glass Sasha works with to make her stained-glass creations. Installing the faucet and taps through the mirror saves counter space—and it looks really cool and ultra-modern.

ABOVE: The look here is clean and contemporary, tempered by traditional touches. Dark wood grounds the space and sets off the crisp, white quartz vanity cover and multitoned backsplash. Crystal vanity handles and knobs nod to the glass theme that plays throughout the room. Chrome sconces with fabric shades interpret traditional style in a modern material.

WORTH THE CLIMB

CHALLENGE

Trish and her family bought this house largely because of the extra space afforded by the attic master bedroom and bath. But the attic renovation was 25 years old and it desperately needed updating. The bedroom had lots of light and a vaulted ceiling, but the bathroom/ dressing area was a spooky warren of dark, chopped-up spaces with low and oddly angled ceilings. The dingy shower felt cramped and old, and an unused bidet just got in the way. Another big negative for Trish was the absence of a tub. She longed for a big, open, spalike space full of beautiful light—with a luxury tub perfect for soaking and relaxing!

Backsplash

Vinyl flooring

Bedside tables

Wall color

BEFORE: An attic renovation 25 years earlier had carved the bathroom half of the suite into a dark warren of nooks, crannies, and awkward spaces. There was a dingy, dated shower but no tub, and the bidet was simply in the way.

AFTER: The soaring ceiling in the bedroom now continues into the bath, creating a much more spacious feeling. I left the area above the support beam open to mimic the shape of the gable-end windows and to share light between rooms. A white-on-white color scheme unifies the entire space and makes it feel open, airy, and bright.

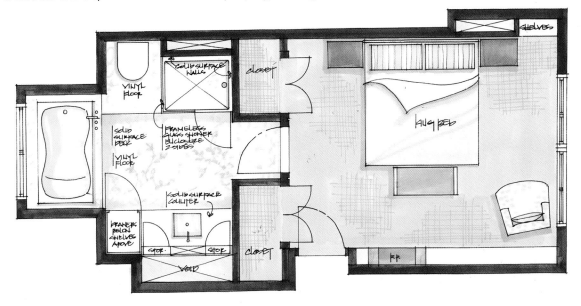

ABOVE: Mirrors create the illusion of endless space in the tub nook, and a frameless glass shower enclosure enhances the feeling of openness. Tile mosaic adds a touch of color to the tub area and shower enclosure.

SOLUTION

- The only cure for Dated Reno Syndrome is to start from scratch, so I knocked out all the walls chopping up the dressing area and bath, tore down the dropped ceilings, and opened the entire space up to the roof.

- With the soaring ceiling now matching the one in the bedroom, I reworked the entry to the bath, centering it under the peak of the roof and creating a sightline from the bed clear through to what would be the new focal point—a beautiful soaker tub tucked into the dormer.

- Reworking the wall of closets so they opened to the bedroom gained some much-needed space for the bath area (see page 169).

- All of the plumbing was relocated and reconfigured to make better use of the space. A huge new glass-and-composite-quartz shower and one-piece toilet occupy one end of the room, and the vanity and storage fill the other end.

- The dormer was big enough to accommodate a 6-foot by 36-inch-wide water-jet tub. On the dormer walls, I installed full-size frameless mirrors above the backsplash to reflect light and to make the two little dormer windows seem to go on ad infinitum.

- A composite quartz countertop on the vanity and glass-tile mosaic on the backsplash make for waterproof, easy-care surfaces in the splash zones. On the floor, vinyl sheet flooring with a small floral motif gives a high-end look at low cost.

ABOVE: A unique sink adds instant character to a bath. I chose an unusual wave-shaped porcelain sink here to add a bit of modern flair.

RIGHT: To give Trish a luxurious spa experience in the shower, I included a rain shower head along with a flexible handheld shower head for directed spray.

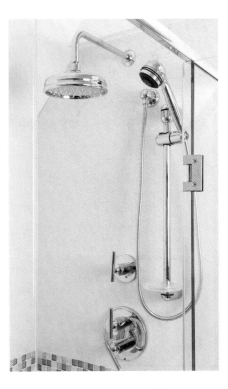

STYLE ELEMENTS

- With any attic renovation, you're dealing with a multitude of angles, and this is not the place to introduce a complicated mix of colors on walls and ceilings. Instead, I used a white-on-white scheme that allows the light to bounce off surfaces and define the architecture with a play of light and shadow.

- All-white fixtures and cabinetry reinforce this scheme and help create a light, bright, airy feeling. Polished chrome faucets add more sparkle.

- To bring in the cooling spa colors Trish wanted, I chose a beautiful glass-tile mosaic with squares of soothing aqua, cream, and shades of green.

- Bathrooms are full of hard, shiny, cold surfaces, so it's important to introduce some touchable textures for warmth. A big cocoa-color rug and matching towels add texture and a dark neutral color, accenting all the clean, crisp white.

- With the ceiling raised to the roofline, recessed ceiling lights weren't an option, so I had track lighting installed along the beam that supports the ceiling between the bedroom and the bath.

- To tie the bedroom into the new bathroom scheme, I repainted the walls to match the bath and attached an upholstered headboard to the wall to give the bed more presence. The platform bed got a coat of white paint, new white bedding, and pillows in restful cocoa, white, and robin's-egg blue.

BEFORE: Taupe walls created a surprisingly dark environment in the attic suite, and the platform bed lacked presence or importance.

ABOVE: Fresh white paint on the walls, ceiling, and platform bed brought the bedroom in line with the new bath. The closets now open into the bedroom, gaining precious space for the expanded bath.

4 RELAXING RETREATS

MODERN BLEND

CHALLENGE

The itsy-bitsy bath in this 1900s home just couldn't handle the demands of a twenty-first-century family. It had no storage space for the myriad toiletries and linens a family needs, and each morning was a battle of jockeying for shower and sink time! Homeowner Alissa was willing to steal space from an adjoining dressing room, but the problem was that Alissa is a self-confessed clotheshorse and dreaded the idea of losing precious closet space. I had to find a way to expand the space-challenged bath and find a home for her beloved wardrobe too!

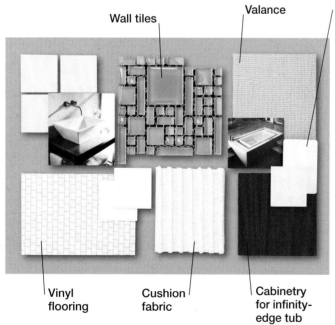

Wall tiles

Valance

Solid surfacing

Vinyl flooring

Cushion fabric

Cabinetry for infinity-edge tub

BEFORE: This teeny-tiny, elderly bathroom (with no storage space) shared a plaster-and-lath wall with a dressing room that inefficiently housed a portion of Alissa's vast collection of clothing.

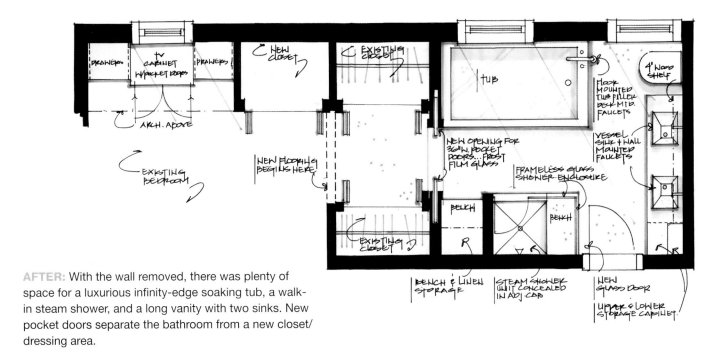

DRAWERS | TV CABINET W/POCKET DOORS | DRAWERS

NEW CLOSET

EXISTING CLOSET

TUB

FLOOR MOUNTED TUB FILLER DECK MTD. FAUCETS

4" WOOD SHELF

ARCH. ABOVE

EXISTING BEDROOM

NEW FLOORING BEGINS HERE

NEW OPENING FOR 36"W. POCKET DOORS...FROST FILM GLASS

VESSEL SINK & WALL MOUNTED FAUCETS

FRAMELESS GLASS SHOWER ENCLOSURE

EXISTING CLOSET

BENCH

BENCH

R

R

R

BENCH & LINEN STORAGE

STEAM SHOWER UNIT CONCEALED IN ADJ CAP

NEW GLASS DOOR

UPPER & LOWER STORAGE CABINET

AFTER: With the wall removed, there was plenty of space for a luxurious infinity-edge soaking tub, a walk-in steam shower, and a long vanity with two sinks. New pocket doors separate the bathroom from a new closet/ dressing area.

SOLUTION

- I started by knocking out the wall between the tiny bath and the dressing room to create one large space. I carved out a new, better organized closet/dressing room and installed pocket doors for privacy. To take care of Alissa's clothing collection, I reorganized the existing walk-in closet in the master bedroom and converted an awkward corner into another small closet.

- Under the window of the old dressing room, I installed the most luxurious soaking tub I could find. Water flows over the infinity edge, allowing for complete immersion. And with the push of a button, Alissa can activate bubble jets to soothe away the stress of the day or chromatherapy lights to alter her mood. The idea behind chromatherapy is that color affects your energy level—so red, for example, invigorates, while blue or green induces calm.

- For everyday showering, I put in a new walk-in steam shower with a built-in bench, all in marble composite. The frameless glass shower enclosure helps keep the room feeling open.

- Along the wall where the old bathtub had been, I installed a beautiful new vanity with two sinks—no more competing for sink time!

- In place of the old toilet, I brought in a glamorous new hatbox commode. All of the working parts are enclosed within the sleek, oval shape, and its electric flushing system is super-efficient. And best of all, it has an automatic quiet-close seat. Ladies, do we love that?!

- An elegant pearlescent vinyl floor tile replaced the old miniature mosaic tiles with the look of inlaid mother-of-pearl.

- To really take this bathroom to the next level of luxury, I had the room wired for sound and video. Water-resistant speakers set into the ceiling pipe Alissa's favorite tunes into the shower and over the tub. An MP3 docking station in the new walk-in closet can be programmed and controlled with a keypad or a remote. And where is the video, you ask? Check the mirror! Great for catching up on the morning news while getting ready or for winding down at night with your favorite drama while soaking in the tub.

ABOVE: It's the latest thing in contemporary commodes—an electric-flush hatbox toilet with a seat that closes automatically. Don't you love it?!

ABOVE: Vessel sinks look like modern sculpture, and green glass tile set in a geometric pattern adds color and a touch of retro design.

ABOVE: With two sinks and mirrors, Alissa and her partner can get ready for work at the same time, and there's no more scrambling for storage space with the generous vanity. Pendants and recessed accent lights illuminate the sink area for grooming and makeup tasks. Perfectly positioned for the tub, the left mirror incorporates an LCD TV that disappears when turned off. When on, it's hooked up to cable and controlled by remote. Bring on the popcorn!

STYLE ELEMENTS

- I chose dark wood to set a modern tone, but the wood does double duty—it also takes the hard edge off the contemporary design and warms it up.

- For the high contrast that makes a modern scheme crisp and clean, I used a mottled cream-color stone composite for the countertop, tub decking, and shower enclosure. Gorgeous green glass tile laid in a retro-inspired pattern adds a splash of color to the walls in the wet zones and gives a nod to the historic character of the house.

- At the windows, I hung traditional wooden blinds for privacy and light control. To add some softness and color, I topped the windows with tailored, pleated valances that pick up the colors of the tile and the composite countertop.

- Vessel sinks with wall-mounted lever faucets look like functional sculpture, reinforcing the sleek, modern feel.

OPPOSITE: The walk-in steam shower features a water-resistant, ceiling-mounted speaker hooked into the sound system. Singing in the shower never sounded better! Vinyl flooring looks like inlaid mother-of-pearl for an elegant, neutral finish underfoot.

ABOVE: For a little bit of fun and sparkle over the soaker tub, I hung this lighted silver-wire ball—it looks kind of like a stylized paperclip collection! Pleated valances hide the mechanics of wooden blinds at the windows and add a bit of color at ceiling height.

LEFT: Frosted-glass panels in the pocket door dividing the master bath from Alissa's new closet give the room a greater feeling of openness and light while preserving privacy.

CHIC BOUTIQUE STYLE

CHALLENGE

First-time home buyer Barnaby had jumped head-first into a total renovation but now he was facing a gutted house, flagging energy, and renovation fatigue. He hoped that if I could help him with the bathroom, it might put him back on track for tackling the rest of the house. Trouble was, the existing bathroom was a tiny 3×5-foot space that held little promise. Barnaby wanted a cool, modern bathroom with a bit of boutique hotel vibe, but he wasn't sure how to make that happen.

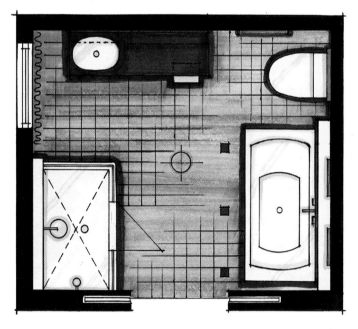

BEFORE: Originally a guest room, this would become Barnaby's new luxury master bath. The door got walled in, the popcorn ceiling pulled down, and the wall between this room and the adjoining, postcard-size bathroom torn out to make one big space.

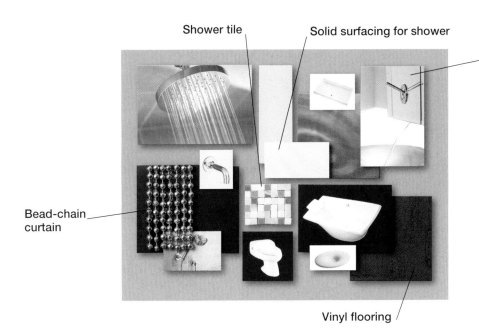

Shower tile

Solid surfacing for shower

High-tech medicine chest

Bead-chain curtain

AFTER: Gorgeous fixtures, elegant finishes, and an understated palette of cool grays, snowy white, and dark walnut create a modern, masculine space that feels warm, relaxing, and comfortable. Easy-care seamless vinyl flooring in a pewter finish mimics tile, giving a high-end look at an affordable price.

Vinyl flooring

SOLUTION

- Fortunately, there was a guest bedroom between the tiny bathroom and the future master bedroom, so with a little demolition work, I took down the wall between the bath and the guest room and created one big space. I also widened the doorway and installed space-saving pocket doors.

- A shower to the left of the door and a sculptural freestanding tub on the right took care of the two must-have fixtures for a boutique bathroom. I chose frameless glass walls for the shower to keep the space feeling wide open and bright and fitted it with a luxurious rain shower head as well as a hand shower.

- Beside the tub, a toilet with a bidet seat and remote-controlled self-closing mechanism offers the latest in bathroom technology. Très chic!

- Sightlines were important in this space, so I put a beautiful vanity with a gorgeous vessel sink directly opposite the door. It's the first thing anyone sees on entering or passing by. On the wall above, I installed a high-tech medicine cabinet that incorporates the faucet. How cool is that?! On either side, a slim panel pulls out to reveal lighted shelving.

- For flooring, I chose sheet vinyl in an elegant metallic finish. Vinyl is great for bathrooms because it's completely seamless, waterproof, easy to maintain, and comes in a zillion textures and colors. This one is scored to look like 6×6-inch tile, giving high style for a low price.

- I wanted a mosaic tile feature to give visual interest and color to the shower and tub walls and found a ¼-inch marble tile that would pull everything together. The walls below the tile are covered with quartz composite for a clean, serene, splash-proof surface.

LEFT: A vinyl graphic made from a greatly enlarged photo of a water drop turns the ceiling into a decorative feature. I added a small bulkhead around the perimeter of the ceiling to house recessed lighting.

OPPOSITE: Landscape lighting set into the floor throws light onto the tub, emphasizing its graceful, sculptural shape. A quartz-clad half-wall contains the plumbing and provides a ledge for display or toiletries. The custom-built cabinet above the toilet is studded with upholstery tacks to pick up the beaded-chain window treatment (see page 183).

STYLE ELEMENTS

- To create the sophisticated, elegant feeling you'd find in a modern boutique hotel, I chose a color palette of grays, blues, and snowy white. Dove-gray walls and pewter flooring contrast with the pure white quartz "wet walls" and fixtures. The mosaic tile pulls the colors together with a random graphic pattern of white and shades of gray.

- Dark wood looks great against a neutral palette and adds warmth to the space, so I chose a graceful, modern vanity in dark walnut. Its wavy, organic shape picks up on the sculptural curves of the tub as well as the beautiful, vaselike shape of the sink. And it's not just a pretty face—the drawer provides storage for toiletries and is even fitted with an electrical outlet for a razor or hair dryer. The stool is pretty fun, too—the seat comes off to reveal a wastebasket, and the entire stool scoots around on ball bearings in the base!

- The existing window was small, but instead of replacing it, I found a unique and very stylish way to disguise it without blocking the light: beaded chains that slide onto a ceiling-mounted track. I had them trimmed just above the floor to create a drapery effect that's very masculine and avant-garde and adds a bit of shimmer to the room.

- Fantastic lighting is key to giving this space its chic, modern character. To play up the sculptural quality of the tub, I had low-voltage, waterproof landscape lights installed in the floor to up-light the tub. The real "wow" factor, though, comes from the ceiling, where I had a shallow bulkhead built to house recessed lighting. In the trough around the perimeter, hidden halogen spotlights wash the walls with light, and in the center a sleek ceiling fixture seems to emerge from the mural—a dramatically enlarged photo of a water drop printed on graphic vinyl.

LEFT: Plumbing for the sink is inside the super-cool high-tech medicine chest, with the faucet and lever control projecting from the mirror. The side sections of the mirror pull out to reveal lighted shelving.

OPPOSITE: The frameless glass shower virtually disappears, making the most of the beautiful mosaic tile as a decorative feature. Beaded chain hangs from a ceiling-mounted track to disguise the window and add luscious shimmer. Yummy!

RELAXATION THERAPY

CHALLENGE

As medical professionals with one young child, Grant and Ayesha lead busy, stress-filled lives. They wanted to come home to a master bath that's restful, relaxing, and rejuvenating—a place to shed the cares of the day. Instead, they had a 1980s eyesore, with acres of green marble, wall-size mirrors, little storage, and blinding makeup lights over the vanity. The tub—raised on a platform with steps—aimed at grandeur but missed the mark. The shower, on the other hand, was cramped and dark and seemed like an afterthought. Rx? One therapeutic renovation to take this bathroom from frumpy to fabulous!

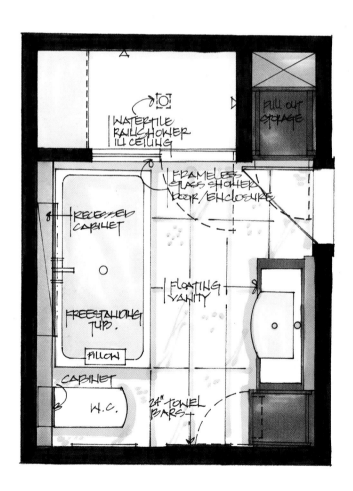

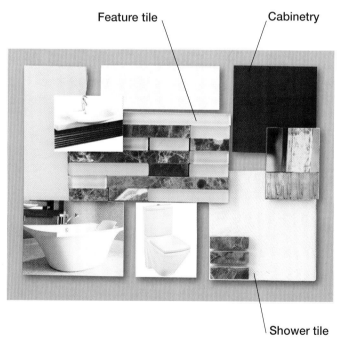

Feature tile

Cabinetry

Shower tile

BEFORE: Miles of green tiles and acres of mirror made this 1980s bathroom feel harsh and uncomfortable. With lots of wasted space, too-bright vanity lighting, and a dark, cramped shower, it didn't relieve stress—it caused it!

AFTER: With a linen closet where the shower used to be and a spectacular walk-in shower where the tub once sat, the renovated bath is a deluxe therapy room for homeowners Grant and Ayesha. The glass walls of the shower make the room feel bigger, even though we stayed within the original footprint.

ABOVE: A graceful sink resting on a fluted slab of wenge wood floats against the wall of mosaic tile. A minimalist vanity like this actually increases the illusion of space in the room. To make the most of the custom cupboard's storage capacity, I fitted it with wire and woven baskets that help keep toiletries organized.

OPPOSITE: The vanity front pulls out to reveal a sectioned drawer for toiletries and cosmetics.

SOLUTION

- At 90 square feet, the bathroom had plenty of space, but much of it was wasted. To create a better layout, I tore out all of the mirrors, marble, cabinetry, and fixtures and started from scratch.

- Two elements no relaxing bathroom can do without: a really good shower and a pampering tub. I installed a spectacular shower where the old space-eating tub had been. Fully adjustable body-spray tiles on the wall, a rain shower tile overhead, and a hand shower beside the built-in bench allow for a made-to-order shower experience. On the adjacent wall, a beautiful free-standing soaker tub with a wall-mounted faucet promises to soothe away stress. Just what the doctor ordered!

- On the wall behind the tub, I wanted a focal point feature that said "Wow, look at me!" and I found it in a gorgeous tile mosaic that mixes marble strips with glass tiles. It covers the entire wall behind the tub as well as the lower half of the opposite wall, where it sets off the vanity.

- With the mosaic tile as a jumping-off point, I chose 12×24-inch large-format porcelain tiles for the floor and shower enclosure. The contrast in scale between the large-format porcelain and the slender strips of mosaic creates a stunning effect—expansive, calming shapes versus eye-catching detail.

- A new vanity in dark wenge wood houses a sink that's a graceful, sculptural piece echoing the lines of the tub.

- Since lack of storage had been a problem in the old bathroom, I included lots of new storage in the renovation. The old shower became a new linen closet, complete with a pull-out laundry basket, and I added a floor-to-ceiling cabinet beside the sink, a shallow cupboard tucked between the studs over the toilet, and a recessed niche above the tub.

- A sleek, dual-flush toilet looks elegant and saves water—push one button for a little water, push the other when you need more.

STYLE ELEMENTS

- The marble-and-glass mosaic offered a prescription for color as well as scale: cocoa-brown tiles for the floor, creamy tiles for the shower, and chocolate-color wenge for the cabinetry.

- Creamy paint on the walls and trim matches the porcelain tiles in the shower enclosure and balances the dark tones.

- A wall-mounted towel heater not only warms and dries towels but can also be used to air-dry delicates and make baby blankets toasty.

- Lighting is key in the new space. Sconces mounted through the vanity mirror provide light for grooming, while recessed ceiling fixtures wash walls with ambient light. In the shower, water-resistant fixtures in the base of the bench provide soft, intimate lighting. And the ceiling fixture—amplified by the light that comes through the glass doors—guarantees no more showering in the dark!

RIGHT: A free-standing sculptural soaker tub against a mosaic tile wall makes a stunning focal point for the room. A custom-built niche offers handy tubside storage and display, and a shallow cabinet tucked between the studs adds more storage over the elegant new dual-flush toilet. For luscious luxury, I hung an electric towel warmer on the wall. Mmm, fluffy warm towels.

GENTLEMEN'S CLUB

CHALLENGE

The bathroom/dressing area on the third floor of Henry and Nick's Victorian row house may be one of the most bizarre "re-muddled" spaces I've ever encountered! A previous owner had created a strange labyrinth with a sunken tub, a cramped enclosed shower, a mirrorless vanity, and a closet that eventually led to the toilet. Henry and Nick wanted a true master bath suite and dressing area that would feel like a gentlemen's club—classic, elegant, and tranquil. And because Henry was committing to a new exercise regimen, they also asked me to build in a convenient workout area. No small order!

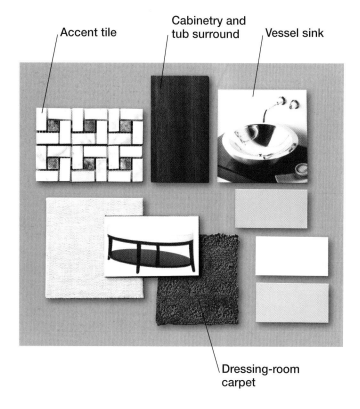

Accent tile

Cabinetry and tub surround

Vessel sink

Dressing-room carpet

BEFORE: This oddly configured third-floor master bath defied functionality, with the vanity, sunken tub, and cramped shower clustered in the center of a labyrinth of small rooms.

AFTER: The new bathroom is open and airy with clearly defined functional zones. An inlaid mosaic "rug" adds visual interest to the clean, white tile floor, which flows seamlessly into the shower for a barrier-free design.

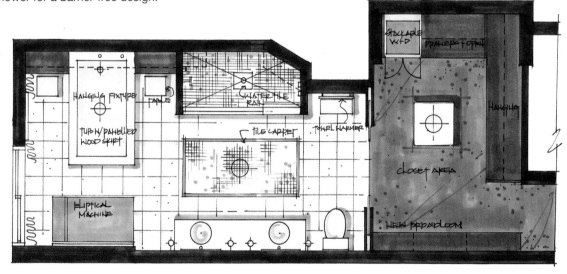

SOLUTION

- Once the maze of small rooms and chaotic construction was gutted, I laid out an efficient, functional floor plan. At the head of the stairs, I placed a roomy, luxurious closet/dressing room, which is separated from the bathroom by frosted-glass doors.

- In the bathroom, I placed a barrier-free shower stall with a huge frameless glass enclosure on one wall and outfitted it with body-spray tiles, a rain shower head, and hand shower. "Barrier-free" means the flooring continues seamlessly into the shower with the floor angled slightly to promote drainage. The end effect is not only a shower that is more modern and sleek looking but also easier to clean.

- The toilet and a vanity with twin sinks and mirrors line up on the opposite wall. A thick quartz countertop wraps the vanity for a modern feel. Sleek, stainless-steel sinks with wall-mounted spout faucets emphasize the minimalist, spa look.

- At the end of the room, a deep soaker tub creates an elegant focal point, with a waterproof LCD TV built into the wall. Cool or what?! Beautiful, custom-built bookcases flank the tub to play up the gentlemen's club atmosphere—definitely not your usual bathroom furniture!

- For flooring, I chose water-resistant tile with a radiant-heat pad underneath to take off the chill in winter.

- With an elliptical trainer positioned to take advantage of the outdoor view or the TV, Henry can start his exercise regimen in style. The new sliding glass doors have integrated shades for privacy and will eventually open to a new balcony.

- The new closet system would be the envy of any fashionista. Shelves, drawers, double-hanging bars, a built-in ironing board, and a stacked washer/dryer offer the absolute maximum in organization, order, and efficiency (see pages 196–197).

LEFT: Bookcases flanking the soaker tub help take this space from utilitarian to elegant, creating the feeling of an exclusive club room. A waterproof LCD TV set into the wall also has a waterproof remote, handy for TV watching while soaking tired muscles after a vigorous workout.

ABOVE: This super-deluxe shower includes adjustable body-spray tiles that shoot water horizontally and diagonally—so you can shower without getting your head wet! Or, if you want a head-to-toe drenching, there's the rain shower head that sends water cascading from above. And for directed spray (or cleaning the shower), the removable hand-held shower head is ideal.

STYLE ELEMENTS

- Creating a masculine space starts with dark wood, and achieving a gentlemen's club look calls for some furniture-style elements. Using walnut-stained wood, I designed a vanity that looks like a dresser, a paneled tub surround, and the pair of floor-to-ceiling, wall-hugging bookcases. Wrapping the vanity in white quartz emphasizes modern, minimalist lines, making for a tranquil and relaxing space.

- To balance the dark tones, I contrasted them with snowy white floors, countertops, toilet, and tub. The quartz and tile have no pattern in them at all, which helps foster a calm feeling in the room.

- Warm gray walls embrace the room in soothing, quiet color and make an understated backdrop for the dark wood tones and crisp white features.

- For visual interest, I chose a mosaic tile of white natural stone with a dark taupe insert. Used on the tub wall, shower niche, and an inlaid floor "rug," the mosaic adds touches of pattern and contrasting scale to draw attention to the room's three key areas—the vanity, the shower, and the tub.

- Four beautiful chrome sconces with shades flank the mirrors above the sinks. Inspired by torches, they blend a traditional shape with a pared-down, streamlined attitude. Along with the stainless-steel sinks, they bring in a bit of contemporary sparkle to balance the warm wood. Over the tub, I hung a glittery chandelier of chrome discs to highlight this fabulous feature area.

- This room is all about luxury, so naturally I had to include a towel heater beside the shower! Jeeves, where's my towel?

- To add some softness, chic white linen curtains with extra-large grommets frame the sliding glass doors.

OPPOSITE: Built to look like a dresser, the vanity has faux drawers in the center and real ones on either side. I wrapped the piece in thick white quartz for a crisp, contemporary look. Stainless-steel vessel sinks and chrome sconces emphasize the modern vibe.

LEFT: The frameless mirror rises from the countertop to catch the reflection of this fantastic sink and wall-mount spout faucet. Each mirror is mounted over a ¾-inch-thick wood panel to give it substance. The electric towel warmer occupies a niche dictated by the house's architecture.

LEFT: A complete closet system in dark wood brings the masculine feel of the bathroom into the dressing room. The stacked washer and dryer hide behind the cabinet doors on the left.

ABOVE: Ah, the serenity of a perfectly ordered closet! Shoe racks and shelves for folded items tailored this storage system to Henry and Nick's fashionable needs.

THE ULTIMATE WET ROOM

CHALLENGE

The bathroom in this 1920s home felt teeny-tiny to Rex and Bob, who not only had to share the bathroom with each other but also with two pony-size Great Danes! A small tub with a broken shower door and absolutely no storage other than the windowsill added to the awkwardness and complete lack of function. Bob wanted lots of storage and Rex, a world-renowned ballet dancer, needed a steam shower and soaker tub where he could unwind after a performance. And for the real prima donnas in this household, we needed an easy bathing spot to keep them looking their doggie best!

EXISTING WINDOW

BUBBLE MASSAGE TUB W/ CHROMATHERAPY

BENCH FORMS WET TABLE

WALL HUNG TOILET CARILLET

HATBOX TOILET

STEAM SHOWER GENERTH ABOVE STORAGE CAB!

CONSOLE LAVATORY

FROSTED GLASS FRENCH DOORS!

BEFORE: This basic bathroom was seriously out of date, lacked storage, and was too small for two adults and two huge Great Danes.

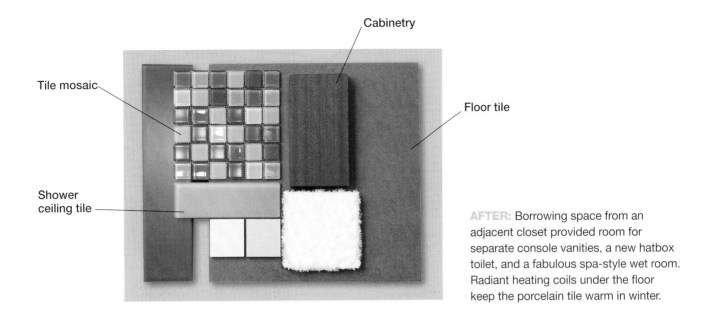

Tile mosaic

Cabinetry

Floor tile

Shower
ceiling tile

AFTER: Borrowing space from an adjacent closet provided room for separate console vanities, a new hatbox toilet, and a fabulous spa-style wet room. Radiant heating coils under the floor keep the porcelain tile warm in winter.

SOLUTION

- To give Rex and Bob a bath big enough to pirouette in, I had to find more space. Fortunately, an adjacent closet that had been dismantled could be incorporated into the new bathroom, so I tore out one wall as well as fixtures, flooring, and even the decrepit old window.

- In the space where the old bathroom had been, I designed a fantastic wet room with a spectacular steam shower and a built-in air-massage tub with chromatherapy lights. The shower includes body sprays, hand shower, rain shower heads, and steam to offer every option imaginable. (The hand shower is particularly handy for washing down big dogs!)

- For waterproof, easy-care surfaces throughout the wet room, I wrapped the entire space in tile—a small multi-tone tile mosaic for the walls, larger glass tiles for the ceiling, and porcelain tiles for the floor and tub face. To make the space completely watertight, I installed waterproofing membrane throughout the room before the tiles were applied. I also laid radiant heating under the porcelain tile floor to keep toes and paws toasty in winter.

- Even the new windows are moisture-proof, combining a fiberglass composite frame with frosted glass for privacy. The windows not only admit light—they're also part of the ventilation system that lets steam escape. The other escape route is a transom in the shower door, with a ceiling vent just outside it.

- To give Rex an at-home spa experience worthy of a five-star resort, I designed a very special bench. It looks like nesting tables, but pull out the lower table and you have a proper chaise. Three rain shower heads in the ceiling cascade water down on over the chaise for a phenomenally relaxing experience. Aaahhh, bliss!

- With the wet room dedicated to all things water-related, I designed the rest of the space for function—sinks, toilet, and storage. Rex and Bob specifically requested separate sinks, so I selected two console vanities, one to go on either side of the bathroom. A tall wall-hung medicine cabinet on one side and a floor-to-ceiling cabinet on the other provide tons of storage for all kinds of toiletries.

- A beautiful hatbox toilet with a high-efficiency electrical flushing system and a self-closing mechanism fits neatly between one vanity and the wet room.

OPPOSITE: Completely covered in tiles, the wet room is thoroughly watertight. Body-spray tiles shoot water or steam. The bench pulls out to form a chaise for unwinding in steamy warmth or enjoying a cascade of water from the ceiling-mounted rain shower heads. Lights set into the tub surround can be dialed down for a more relaxing environment.

RIGHT: Not one but three rain shower heads send down bracing cascades of water for a delicious shower experience. Even the dogs might not mind bathing in a gentle rain shower!

OPPOSITE: On the wall opposite the body stray tiles, I installed a hand-held shower head to handle quick, "ordinary" showers. It's great for washing big dogs, too!

ABOVE: The air-massage soaker tub includes chromatherapy lights that suffuse the water with mood-enhancing color. The big bonus with air-massage versus water-massage tubs is that they circulate air rather than tub water, allowing you to use all of your favorite bath gels, lotions, and potions without concern that they will clog the mechanics of the system.

ABOVE: The style meter goes way over the top with sleek console vanities, contemporary cabinetry, and open shelving. Chrome and leather legs support thick porcelain sinks with super-wide sides, perfect for keeping essentials close at hand.

STYLE ELEMENTS

- To create a soothing yet masculine feeling in the room, I chose a color scheme of browns, sage green, and gray, with crisp white accents. The ¼-inch mosaic glass tile for the wet room walls provided the springboard for the other elements and pulls them all together.

- This bathroom has *a lot* of tile, and to keep it from feeling overwhelming, I varied the sizes and shapes—long rectangular tiles on the ceiling, squares set in a diamond pattern on the floor, and large-format porcelain tiles on the tub face and the floor outside the wet room.

- To create the contemporary look Rex and Bob wanted, I chose vanities with sleek, leather-accented polished chrome legs. The pieces are visually light and structurally open, enhancing the room's feeling of spaciousness.

- Lighting addresses function as well as mood-setting ambience in this chic, resort-style bath. While recessed ceiling lights supply overall light, task lighting comes from style-setting, specially designed sconces that hang at eye level for perfect, nonglare, no-shadow illumination for grooming. Landscaping lights set into the side of the tub are on a dimmer switch for perfect mood control.

ABOVE: Specially designed sconces bring to mind car-hood ornaments and have a suitably modern masculine vibe.

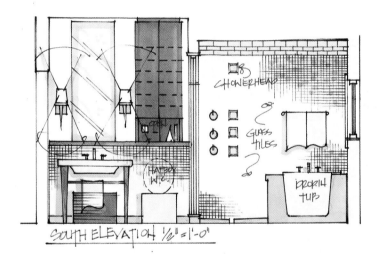

SOUTH ELEVATION ½"=1'-0"

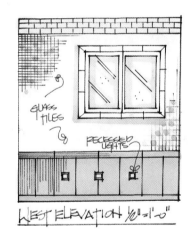

WEST ELEVATION ½"=1'-0"

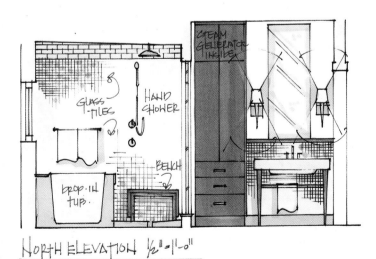

NORTH ELEVATION ½"=1'-0"

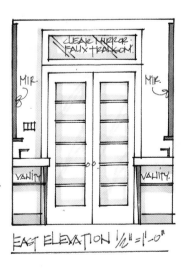

EAST ELEVATION ½"=1'-0"

PARENTS' TIME OUT

CHALLENGE

With three small children and a newborn, where can a busy mom— or dad—go to relax and recharge? For Tonia and Francis, it definitely was *not* their cramped and cluttered bathroom, with its peeling striped wallpaper, grungy tub, and awkward layout. Tonia longed for a serene, contemporary bath where they could start and end the day in a relaxing and refreshing environment. Key components would include a luscious soaker tub for her and a fabulous shower for Francis—he loved the idea of a home shower with the spray-from-every-direction effect of a car wash!

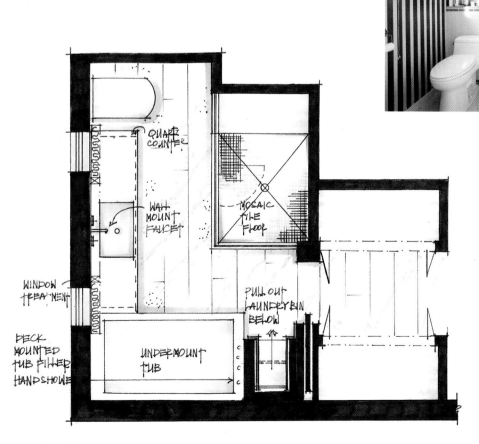

BEFORE: With peeling wallpaper, cracked tile, and a grungy tub, this bathroom was a long way from the relaxing, refreshing oasis Tonia and Francis wanted. The only storage space for toiletries was along a ledge above the toilet and pedestal sink.

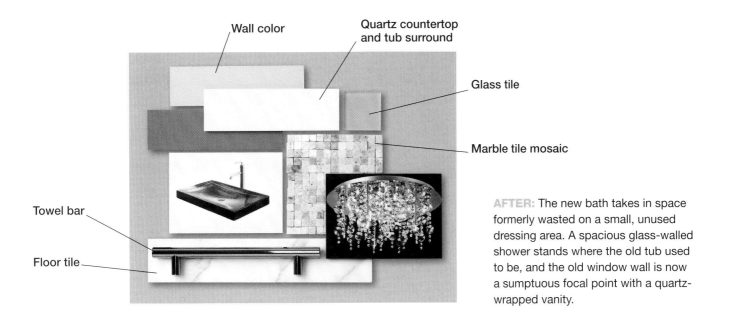

Wall color

Quartz countertop and tub surround

Glass tile

Marble tile mosaic

Towel bar

Floor tile

AFTER: The new bath takes in space formerly wasted on a small, unused dressing area. A spacious glass-walled shower stands where the old tub used to be, and the old window wall is now a sumptuous focal point with a quartz-wrapped vanity.

SOLUTION

- Tonia and Francis never used the small dressing room beside the bath, so it was declared wasted space, and the area was incorporated into the new bathroom footprint. After removing the wall that separated it from the bath, I was left with a relatively large rectangle with two awkwardly placed windows.

- I decided to make the windows part of a focal point wall, with a long vanity underneath. I framed the windows with new woodwork, uniting them with a series of shelves, storage cabinets, and a large mirror, stretching along the wall.

- Beside the vanity, a 24-inch-deep cast-iron soaker tub fills the corner. To give it the look of a contemporary free-standing tub, I installed it in a quartz surround with a wide deck. It's a deep tub and will hold lots of people— but Tonia may not want to share!

- In the sliver of space left between the tub and the wall, I inserted a prefab cabinet with a pull-out laundry drawer. Organization and storage will help keep the bathroom feeling clean and uncluttered—all the better for achieving a relaxing, refreshing mood.

- Where the old tub had been, I installed a huge frameless glass shower with all the bells and whistles—steam shower, body-spray tiles, rain shower head, and a bench. Although the shower takes up a lot of floor space, it doesn't overpower or crowd the room because the glass walls virtually disappear.

- For a waterproof wall covering in the splash zones, I used a ¼-inch marble tile mosaic.

- On the floor, 12×18-inch large-scale Carrara marble tiles lay over a radiant-heat pad, making the floor friendly to feet in winter.

LEFT: A deep-green glass sink rests on the quartz slab countertop like a piece of art. With a sink like this, the faucet and taps are best mounted in the wall.

ABOVE: New mahogany-color woodwork unites the two windows into a custom unit that includes solid and glass-door cabinets and a space-expanding mirror.

STYLE ELEMENTS

- I wanted fresh and soothing colors and materials for Tonia and Francis's parental retreat, and that always means greens or blues. The marble tile mosaic mixes several shades of gray-green with a white Carrara marble tile that matches the large-scale marble tiles on the floor—sweet! The mosaic adds color and fine pattern to the shower and the deep backsplash that wraps the room. It's also the key to other color choices—marine green for the vessel sink and pure white quartz for the shower frame and bench, tub surround, and waterfall vanity countertop.

- Calm, relaxing, cool colors need to be balanced by warmth, and that's where the vanity and storage pieces come in. Mahogany-stained custom cabinetry and a matching prefab storage cabinet weight the lighter colors and turn up the visual thermostat to a comfortable level.

- With the vanity at center stage on the focal-point wall, the sink needed to be spectacular—and it is! A large, rectangular green-glass vessel sink looks like a piece of art.

- This is no ordinary bath, and no ordinary lighting would do. Recessed fixtures wash down the walls and cabinetry for overall lighting. Sconces mounted on the mirror provide task lighting at mid-level, and for a gorgeous focal point over the tub, I chose a flush-mounted chandelier that looks like crystal water drops. It's a contemporary take on a traditional crystal chandelier and will give Tonia something beautiful to gaze at while she soaks away stress.

- For light control and softness, I dressed the two windows in translucent blinds. The coverings diffuse the light to promote a quiet, relaxing feeling—just what Tonia and Francis need at the end of the day!

ABOVE: A prefab storage unit with a pull-out drawer for laundry helps keep the bathroom tidy. We customized it by adding fabric bags embroidered with labels to help with sorting—dry clean or laundry.

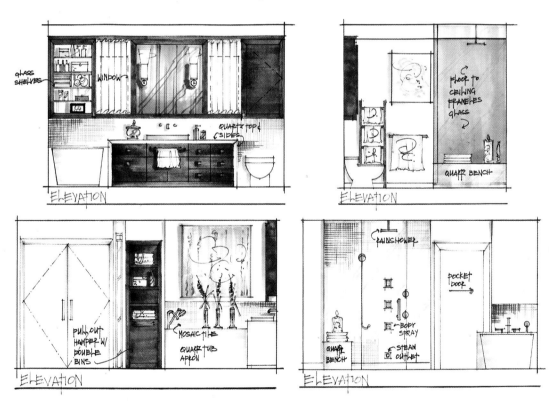

ABOVE: This super-deep soaker tub is under-mounted in a quartz deck and surround to give it the look of a contemporary free-standing tub. Expanses of solid, pattern-free surfaces need some contrast for visual interest, and that's where the mosaic tile comes in. The small tiles introduce color and fine, random pattern to add a bit of liveliness to the space.

ELEGANT UPDATE

CHALLENGE

This run-down family bath had a bad case of the blues—robin's-egg blue, to be exact, with sink, toilet, and tub in matching hues. Sonia's daughter Taryn thought the fixtures were cool and retro, but for Sonia, the bathroom was an embarrassment and an eyesore. The floor tiles were cracked, the shower and rusted baseboard heater didn't work, the toilet needed three flushes to function, and lack of storage space translated into constant clutter. Sonia wanted a modern "grown-up" bath, so we traded something old and blue for something refreshingly new.

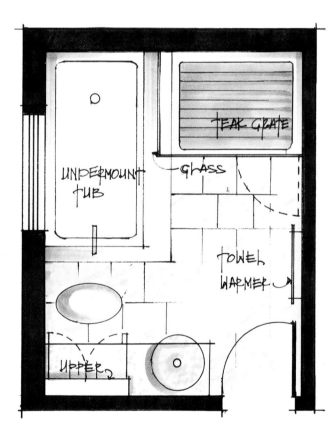

BEFORE: Sonia's daughter put up the blue-and-gold damask wallpaper to persuade her mother that the blue fixtures should stay. But cracking floor tiles, chipped counters, an inefficient toilet, and a nonfunctioning shower tipped the scales toward a complete makeover.

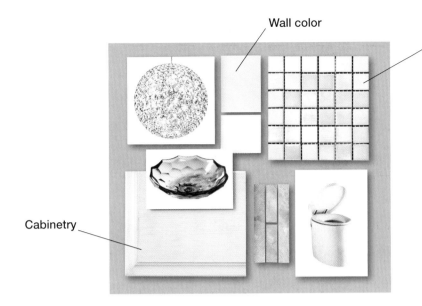

Wall color

Shower-wall mosaic tile

Cabinetry

AFTER: A shimmering wall mural of iridescent tiles turns the back wall of the new bath into a stunning focal point. Clear-glass shower walls allow an unobstructed view of the feature tile and help make the bathroom feel larger. The wide tub deck offers plenty of space for soaps and sponges and serves as a bench inside the shower.

SOLUTION

- First we said good-bye to the monstrous tub and other blue fixtures, as well as the cabinetry, floor tiles, and walls. With new drywall and plumbing lines in place, I positioned a new, smaller tub under the window, opening up floor space for a separate shower. A smaller tub didn't mean less luxury, however. I chose a deep soaker tub with an integrated seat and encased it in a quartz surround with a wide deck—all the comforts of a relaxing soak in an efficiently designed space!

- To make the space feel as large as possible, I designed a walk-in shower with two glass walls. Putting every square inch to work, I extended the shower walls over part of the tub deck to create a bench inside the shower. A teak grate over the cast-iron shower pan gives the unit a cool, spalike look. And to guarantee Sonia's family a spalike experience, I installed both a rain shower head and a hand-held shower that offers four different water options, from relaxing to invigorating.

- The new vanity is shallower than the old one and takes up less floor space but it delivers a lot more storage. A ceiling-height wall cabinet puts previously wasted space to work, and shelves below the countertop go door-less where space is tight. A glass-front cabinet above the toilet also keeps clutter under control.

- I found the perfect toilet to tuck into the small space between the tub and the vanity—a beautiful one-piece fixture with an electric motor that controls the flush.

- To heat the room, I installed an extra-tall wall-mounted towel heater—it not only keeps towels toasty, but it also warms the room comfortably.

- Marble floor tiles make a fresh, crisp background for the new room and visually help open up the small space.

ABOVE: A beautiful cut-glass vessel sink distinguishes the narrow vanity. Mirror-mounted faucet and taps are clean, contemporary—and space-saving.

OPPOSITE: A space-saving tankless toilet tucks in between the tub and vanity. The slender glass-front cabinet has glass shelves and mirror backing for a light and airy look.

STYLE ELEMENTS

- The bathroom's back wall is the first thing you see when you enter, so I wanted to make it a stunning feature. I found just the thing for a style-setting mural: a gorgeous mosaic of ½-inch pearlized tiles in a stylized damask pattern.

- The subtle colors in the iridescent tile inspired the choice of marble floor. The tiles, which have an undertone of green, also suggested the wall paint, tinted with a whisper of spa green.

- To give the new bath a clean, modern look, I chose contemporary custom cabinetry in a light, bright maple finish that picks up on a color in the mosaic tile. Minimalist slab-front doors and straight lines maximize the sense of uncluttered space—your eye glides along those crisp edges and smooth surfaces and tells your brain to relax, everything is in order here. Modern acrylic hardware virtually disappears so it doesn't distract from the room's overall clean, refreshing feeling.

- An incredible cut-glass vessel sink sits on the vanity like a diamond—it turns this little space into something extraordinary. To save on counter space, I installed a mirror-mounted faucet and taps above the sink.

- For some glitter and glamour over the tub, I chose a spectacular crystal pendant sphere. A transparent pendant over the sink, recessed ceiling lights, and a pair of waterproof lights in the side of the tub provide levels of illumination for grooming, showering, or soaking in relaxed bliss.

- Every bath needs a mirror—or two or three. In addition to the ceiling-height mirror over the sink, I installed mirrors at the back of the open and glass-front cabinets, to reflect light and make the room feel larger.

- The small window is the room's only source of natural light, so I covered it with simple vertical blinds sewn from linen and lined with dim-out lining. To give the window more height, I installed a fabric valance just under the ceiling line. With box pleats, piping, and buttons, the valance balances the room's hard surfaces with some tailored softness.

OPPOSITE: Custom maple cabinetry provides a mix of open and closed storage to help keep clutter under control. Open shelves below the quartz countertop solve the problem of too little space for cabinet doors. Mirrors make the room feel larger.

INDEX

A

Appliance garage, 19

Appliances. *See specific appliances by name*

Artichoke lamp, 82

Attic master suite, 164–169

B

Backsplash

basketweave pattern, 20

giving space character, 144

glass mosaic, 24–25, 67, 89

glass tile, 39–40, 98, 120, 126

herringbone pattern, 34

L-shaped kitchen, 19

marble mosaic, 56

marble tile, 60, 112

mirrored, 92

soapstone mosaic tile, 107

stainless-steel, 136

stretcher bond pattern, 40

Baker's kitchen, 134–141

Banquette seating, 43, 44, 50

Bar chairs, 26, 64, 94, 132

Bar stools, 18

Bathtubs. *See* Tubs

Beverage center, 56, 92, 113

Blinds

translucent, 210

vertical, 216

wood, 176

woven, 60, 67, 71, 88, 154–155

Bookcases, bathroom, 192, 194–195

Buffet, 20, 132–133

C

Cabinetry

contemporary, bathroom, 204

custom maple, bathroom, 216–217

dark cherry finish, 34

floor-to-ceiling, 132

furniture-style, 105

mahogany-stained custom, bathroom, 210

mirror backing, 123

mixing light and dark, 20

pull-out, 33, 120

recessed-panel, 44, 64, 72, 116

Shaker-style, 56, 59, 98, 119–120

slab-front, 89, 126, 136

traditional-style, 34

zebrawood, 81–82

Carrara marble tile, 208–211

Casual contemporary-style kitchen, 142–145

Ceiling fixtures, recessed. *See* Recessed lighting

Chandelier

chrome, 194–195

crystal, 72, 116

crystal-bead, 89

flush-mounted, 210

loft master suite, 154–155

Chic boutique-style bathroom, 178–183

Chromotherapy lights, 200–201, 203

City-style kitchen, 124–129

Closet, 153, 166, 192, 196–197

Coffee maker, built-in, 81–82, 112–113, 120

Console vanity, 199, 204–205

Contemporary-style bathroom, 206–211

Contemporary-style kitchen, 84–90, 130–133, 142–145

Cooktops

chimney-style range hood, 50

electric, 39

induction, 19, 126

integrated, 70

GET MORE DESIGN INSPIRATION FROM
CANDICE OLSON

978-0-696-22584-0 ● $19.95

- 24 dramatic before-and-after room transformations

- Smart tips and practical advice for creating a room that's functional *and* stylish

- Inspiration for applying Candice's creative decorating solutions to your own home